EXPERIMENTS FOR FUTURE
BIOLOGISTS

ROBERT GARDNER
AND JOSHUA CONKLIN

Enslow Publishing
101 W. 23rd Street
Suite 240
New York, NY 10011
USA

enslow.com

Published in 2017 by Enslow Publishing, LLC.
101 W. 23rd Street, Suite 240, New York, NY 10011

Library of Congress Cataloging-in-Publication Data

Names: Gardner, Robert, 1929- author. | Conklin, Joshua, author.
Title: Experiments for future biologists / Robert Gardner and Joshua Conklin.
Description: New York, NY : Enslow Publishing, 2017 | Series: Experiments for future STEM professionals | Includes bibliographical references and index.
Identifiers: LCCN 2016022979 | ISBN 9780766081987 (library bound)
Subjects: LCSH: Biology—Experiments—Juvenile literature.
Classification: LCC QH316.5 .G37 2016 | DDC 570.78—dc23
LC record available at https://lccn.loc.gov/2016022979

Printed in the United States of America

To Our Readers: We have done our best to make sure all website addresses in this book were active and appropriate when we went to press. However, the author and the publisher have no control over and assume no liability for the material available on those websites or on any websites they may link to. Any comments or suggestions can be sent by email to customerservice@enslow.com.

Photo Credits: Cover, Alliance/Shutterstock.com (biologist), i3d/Shutterstock.com (lab), Titov Nikolai/Shutterstock.com (atom symbol), elic/Shutterstock.com (green geometric background throughout book), Zffoto/Shutterstock.com (white textured background throughout book), p. 54 stihii/Shutterstock.com.

Illustrations by Joseph Hill.

CONTENTS

INTRODUCTION

Biology is the study of living organisms. Given the wide array of living organisms and the complexity of each individual organism, biology, as you might imagine, is a diverse field of study.

Biologists are intelligent, imaginative, and creative. They enjoy analyzing and solving problems involving living organisms. We hope this book will help you decide whether you would consider a career in biology.

To prepare for life as a biologist, you should take biology and AP biology as well as chemistry, physics, and all the math courses offered in high school. Also take courses in English and history that require writing because, as a biologist, you will have to write reports about your work and investigations. If you do well in these courses, obtain high scores on your SATs, and perform well during college admissions interviews, you will likely be admitted to a college or university where you can major in biology. To aid in your quest to enter college, you could develop interesting and challenging biology projects for science fairs. These projects will make for lively discussion points when you meet college admissions directors.

Once in college, you can major in biology. You will likely take basic biology, comparative anatomy, physiology, genetics, cell biology, microbiology, botany, embryology, zoology, and other courses. In order to complete your major, other sciences will be required as well. They will likely include inorganic and organic chemistry, physics, computer science, and statistics.

During college, look for opportunities to assist in research. You can often find work at college, local labs, hospitals, government agencies, or even wildlife preserves. Your advisor may be able to help you find such work as a volunteer or as a summer job. During your junior year, make a list of graduate schools that interest you as a candidate for a master's degree or a PhD in biology.

With a BS (Bachelor of Science degree) in biology, you could find a job in industry doing quality control or working as a research assistant. Or you could obtain a master's degree in education and begin a career as a biology teacher at the high school level. However, you might find it more rewarding to continue your education and obtain a PhD. Work for this degree will involve four to five years of coursework and research. You will prepare a thesis under the guidance of a college or university biology professor. A PhD would prepare you to teach and do research at a college or university or in industry.

WHAT DO BIOLOGISTS DO?

Most biologists specialize in one or more of the many fields that require their expertise. Some of those specialties include the following:

Aquatic biologists study the plants and animals found in water. These include microorganisms as well as larger forms of water life. Some are **marine biologists** who investigate organisms that live in salt water, while **limnologists** deal with freshwater organisms.

Biochemists investigate the chemical makeup of living things and have a background in chemistry as well as biology.

Biophysicists are concerned with aspects of life related to physics. They have a good understanding of physics as well as biology.

Botanists investigate plants and the environments in which they live. Some botanists study a variety of plants that include algae, lichens, mosses, ferns, and conifers, as well as flowering plants.

Computational biologists use computer science, mathematics, and statistics to investigate and solve problems or form models to address unsolved issues in biology.

Ecologists investigate the relationships between organisms and the environments in which they exist. They look at population size, pollutants, air quality, soil, water, and other factors to see how they affect life within a particular environment.

Microbiologists work with life that requires a microscope to be seen. They often are involved in research involving viruses, immunology, and human diseases.

Physiologists investigate the life functions of living organisms, both plant and animal, at the cellular and molecular level. They may focus on reproduction, growth, photosynthesis, and other life processes.

Zoologists study animals and wildlife. **Ornithologists** study birds. **Mammologists** study mammals, **herpetologists** investigate reptiles and amphibians, **ichthyologists** study fish, and **entomologists** investigate insects.

THE SCIENTIFIC METHOD

Many biologists are involved in scientific research, looking for answers to questions they have about living things. They ask questions, make careful observations, and conduct research. Different areas of biology use different approaches. Depending on the problem, one method is likely to be more successful than another. Developing a new medicine, finding safer ways to use radiation, or searching for the breeding region of humpback whales requires different techniques, but they all have an understanding of how science is conducted.

Despite the differences, all scientists use a similar general approach while conducting and reporting their experimental research called the scientific method. In most experiments, some or all of the following steps are used: making an observation, formulating a question, making a hypothesis (one possible answer to the question) and a prediction (an if-then statement), designing and conducting one or more experiments, analyzing the results in order to reach conclusions about the prediction, and accepting or rejecting the hypothesis. Scientists share their findings. They write articles about their experiments and their results. Their writings are reviewed by other scientists before being published in journals for wider circulation.

You might wonder how to start an experiment. When you observe something in the world, you may become curious and ask a question. Your question, which could arise from an earlier experiment or from reading, may be answered by a well-designed investigation. Once you have a question, you can make a hypothesis. Your hypothesis is a possible answer to the question (what you think will happen). Once you have a hypothesis, it is time to design an experiment.

In most cases, it is appropriate to do a controlled experiment. This means having two groups that are treated exactly the same except for the single factor being tested. That factor is called a *variable*. For example, suppose your question is: "Will Rhode Island Red chickens lay more eggs eating grain X or grain Y?"

You might hypothesize that chickens fed grain X will lay more eggs than those fed grain Y.

You would establish two groups of the chickens of that species. One group would be fed grain X; an equal number in a second group would be fed an equal quantity of grain Y.

If chickens fed grain X do lay more eggs, your hypothesis would be confirmed. If the chickens fed grain Y lay more eggs, or if both groups lay equal numbers of eggs, your hypothesis would be proven wrong.

Two other terms are often used in scientific experiments—*dependent* and *independent variables*. The dependent variable depends on the value of the independent variable. For example, the area of a plot of land depends on the length and width of the plot. Here, the dependent value is the area. It depends on the length and width, which are the independent variables in this example.

The results of one experiment can lead to a related question. They may send you in a different direction. Whatever the results, something can be learned from every experiment.

BEFORE YOU BEGIN EXPERIMENTING; SOME SUGGESTIONS

At times, as you do the experiments and other activities in this book, you may need a partner. Find someone who likes experimenting as much as you do. In that way, you will both enjoy what you are doing. **If any safety issues or danger is involved in an experiment, you will be warned. In some cases, to avoid danger, you will be asked to work with an adult. Please do so.** We don't want you to take any chances that could lead to an injury.

Like any good scientist, you will find it useful to record your ideas, notes, data, and conclusions in a notebook. By doing so, you can keep track of the information you gather and the conclusions you reach. It will allow you to refer to prior experiments and help you in completing future projects. It may also serve as a reference point during the college admissions process.

SAFETY FIRST

Safety is important when doing science experiments. Some of the rules below may seem obvious to you and others may not, but it is important that you follow all of them.

1. Have an adult help you whenever this book, or any other, so advises.
2. Wear eye protection and closed-toe shoes (not sandals). Tie back long hair.
3. Do not eat or drink while experimenting. Never taste substances being used (unless instructed to do so).
4. Do not touch chemicals with your bare hands. Use tools, such as spatulas, to transfer chemicals from place to place.
5. The liquid in some thermometers is mercury (a dense liquid metal). It is dangerous to touch mercury or breathe mercury vapor. Mercury thermometers have been banned in many states. When doing experiments that require you to measure temperature, use

only electronic or non-mercury thermometers, such as those filled with alcohol. If you have a mercury thermometer in the house, ask an adult if it can be taken to a local thermometer exchange location.

6. Do only those experiments that are described in this book or those that have been approved by an adult.

7. Maintain a serious attitude while conducting experiments. Never fool around or engage in practical jokes.

8. Before beginning an experiment, read all the instructions carefully and be sure you understand them.

9. Remove all items not needed for the experiment from your work space.

10. At the end of every activity, clean all materials used and put them away. Then wash your hands thoroughly with soap and water.

The chapters that follow contain experiments and information that every future young biologist should know. Biology, however, is a vast subject and this book's limited space will allow us to touch only briefly on a few of the ideas and experiments that we trust will give you a sense of what interests you might pursue as a biologist. Let's get to work!

CHAPTER ONE

SOME HUMAN BIOLOGY EXPERIMENTS

We begin with a few experiments that involve you, a living member of the animal kingdom.

EXPERIMENT 1

TAKING A PULSE

How fast is your heart beating? It's easy to find out.

When your heart contracts (beats), it forces blood into and along your arteries. Arteries are elastic. They stretch like a rubber band when more blood is pumped into them. The

THINGS YOU WILL NEED

- **stopwatch**
- **table**
- **clay**
- **soda straw**
- **partner**

expansion of an artery can be felt if the artery is close to the body's surface. What you can feel is called a pulse because the artery pulsates (throbs) as blood is forced through it by the heart.

1. During your visits to a doctor's office, a nurse likely has taken your pulse, but you can also take your own pulse. Put your first two fingers on the underside of your other arm's wrist just beyond the point where your thumb connects with your wrist. (See Figure 1a.)

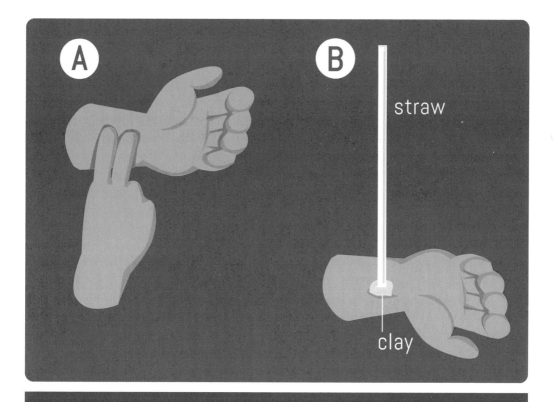

Figure 1. a) A pulse can be felt on the inside of your wrist just behind your thumb. b) You can use a lump of clay and a drinking straw to amplify your pulse and make it visible.

1. Your pulse rate is the number of pulses you feel per minute, but you don't have to count for a full minute. Count the number of pulses for 15 seconds. Then multiply by four to obtain your heart rate in beats per minute.

2. To amplify your pulse and make it visible, put your hand, palm upward, on a table. Put a small lump of clay on the site of your pulse. Stick a straw upright in the clay as shown in Figure 1b. What happens to the straw each time your heart beats?

3. Arteries are close to the surface at other places in your body. A pulse, often used by doctors, is found on either side of your larynx (Adam's apple). There are other pulses just in front of your ear, on the inside of your elbow, and in your ankle. Can you find those pulses?

4. Take a partner's pulse at both his neck and his wrist at the same time. Which pulse do you expect to feel first? Try it! Were you right?

    Your heart is about the size of your fist. It weighs about 290 grams (10.2 ounces). But it is an amazing pump. Each time your heart beats, it pushes about 130 milliliters (4.4 oz) of blood into your arteries.

CIRCULATION OF BLOOD

The human heart, like all mammalian hearts, has four chambers. (See Figure 2.) The two upper chambers are the right and left atria. The lower chambers are the right and left ventricles. Blood returns to the heart from the various parts of the body in veins. The two main veins carrying blood to the right atrium are the superior and inferior vena cava. When the heart muscle contracts, the contraction begins in the atria. The contraction is caused by an electrical signal that starts in the brain and travels through the vagus nerve to the right atrium. The atria contract forcing blood into the right and left ventricles.

Soon after the atria contract, the ventricles contract forcing blood into the pulmonary artery and aorta.

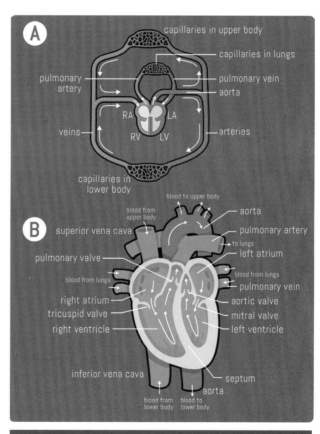

Let's trace a drop of blood as it enters the right atrium. This venous blood has passed close to cells of the body where it has lost much of its oxygen (O_2) while increasing its concentration of carbon dioxide (CO_2). As the heart contracts, the drop of blood, along with other blood, is forced though the tricuspid valve into

Figure 2. a) The general nature of the circulatory system (R = right; L = left; A = atrium; V = ventricle). b) This is a more detailed look at the heart and the vessels leading to it (veins) and from it (arteries).

the right ventricle. As the ventricles contract following the contraction of the atria, the drop is pushed through the pulmonary valve into the pulmonary artery. The pulmonary artery, under pressure from the contracting heart, carries the drop of blood to the lungs. There the artery branches out into smaller arteries that carry blood to all parts of the lung. Eventually the arteries become capillaries. Capillaries are very small vessels with walls so thin that gases dissolved in the blood can pass through them. It is here that the drop of blood picks up O_2 from air in the lungs and transfers its CO_2 to the lung air. The oxygenated drop of blood is transported back to the heart through veins. These veins merge to form the pulmonary vein that brings the blood back to the heart's left atrium.

As the heart contracts, blood passes from the left atrium to the left ventricle through the mitral valve. During the next heart contraction, the blood is pushed from the left ventricle through the aortic valve into the aorta, the body's main artery. The aorta branches into smaller arteries, and the blood eventually reaches capillaries. In the capillaries, O_2 is transferred to body cells and CO_2 moves from cells of the body into the blood. The capillaries come together to form veins that carry blood back to the heart's right atrium.

EXPERIMENT 2

LISTENING TO YOUR HEART

Doctors listen to your heart because it makes meaningful sounds. By listening, they can tell whether or not your heart is behaving normally. Abnormal sounds or rhythms could indicate heart disease or other problems. If you have access to a stethoscope, you can listen to your own and other people's hearts. (A stethoscope is not essential to hear the heart.)

THINGS YOU WILL NEED

- **stethoscope (your family may have one or you could obtain one from medical supply store or science supply house)**
- **a partner**
- **stopwatch**

1. Place the ear tips of a stethoscope in your ears.
2. Put the flat chest piece slightly to the left of the center of your chest. Move the chest piece to slightly different places until you hear the heart sounds loudly and clearly.
3. Listen for two sounds. They occur close together in time. The first sound is longer. The second is a short, sharp sound. Together they sound like "lubb-dup." The "lubb" is caused by the contracting heart muscle

and the closing of the valves between the atria and ventricles. The "dup" is the sound of the aortic and pulmonary valves slamming shut as the heart relaxes after both the atria and ventricles have contracted.

When the heart muscle relaxes, it is no longer pushing the blood. Therefore, the blood tends to flow back into the heart. However, the valves that connect the ventricles to the aorta and pulmonary artery are like the doors to a room. They open only one way—outward, into the aorta and pulmonary artery. When the blood tries to flow back into the heart, the valves slam shut with a loud "dup" sound.

4. If you don't have a stethoscope, you can still hear the sounds. With your partner's permission, place your ear against his chest. (Your partner will probably want to hear your heart as well).

5. Which do you predict should happen first, hearing the heart beat or feeling a pulse in your wrist? Do an experiment to test your prediction.

EXPERIMENT 3

HOW THE HUMAN EYE MAKES THE IMAGES YOU SEE

Your eyes are magnificent sense organs. Figure 3 is a diagram of a cross section of a human eye. Near the front of the eye is a convex lens. The lens, together with the cornea, bends light rays to

THINGS YOU WILL NEED

- **magnifying glass**
- **light-colored wall**
- **window with a view**

form images on the retina at the back of the eye. The retina is rich in nerve cells that respond to light. These nerve cells come together to form the optic nerve, which carries light signals to the brain where we actually see.

1. To see how your lens creates images, you can use a magnifying glass. Magnifying glasses have a convex lens similar to the one in your eye.
2. Hold the lens near a light-colored wall opposite a window with a view.
3. Move the lens back and forth until you see an image on the wall of the view through the window.

A similar thing happens in your eye. The images on your retina, like the one on the wall, are inverted, but you see them as right-side-up.

In an experiment done some time ago, special glasses were made for a person that caused the images on his retina to be right-side-up. He saw them as upside down. After some time, he was able to adjust and see them upright. What do you suppose happened when the special glasses were removed?

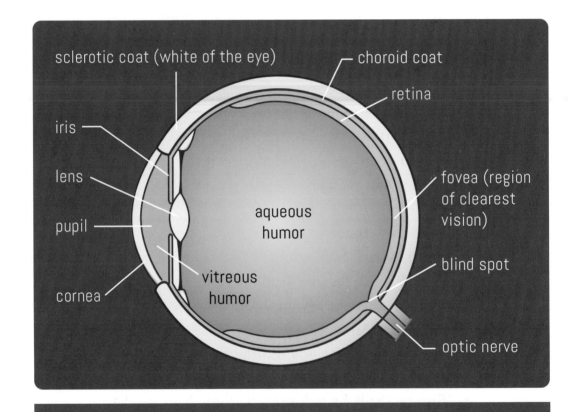

Figure 3. A diagram of the human eye

EXPERIMENT 4

A MODEL OF A CONVEX LENS

You can make a model of a convex lens and see what happens to light rays that pass through the "lens."

THINGS YOU WILL NEED

- **a clear lightbulb such as a tubular showcase bulb with one long vertical filament**
- **clear cylindrical glass or plastic container about 8 centimeters (3 inches) in diameter**
- **water**
- **sheet of white paper**
- **large flat book or magazines**
- **wide hair comb to create light rays**
- **dark room**

1. Set up the model as shown in Figure 4. Nearly fill the container with water.
2. Place the container of water in front of the light source on some white paper resting on a large flat book or magazines. The container of water, which represents a lens, needs to be level with a point near the bottom of the line filament in the clear showcase bulb.
3. Turn on the light and place the comb between the light and the "lens."

4. Notice how the comb divides light from the bulb into rays. What happens to the rays as they enter the "lens"?

   In this model, where would an image form?

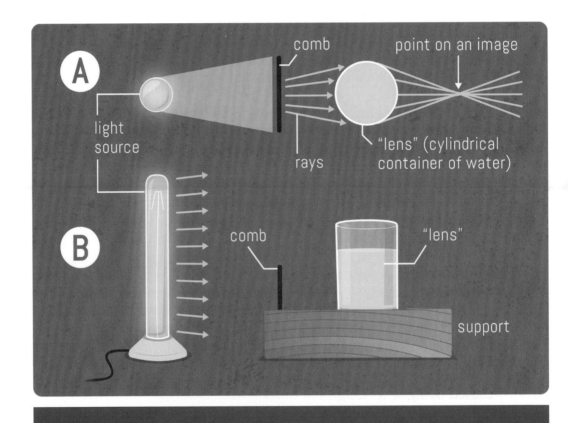

Figure 4. A model of a convex lens: a) overhead view; b) side view

EXPLORING ON YOUR OWN

- Use two convex lenses to make a simple microscope.
- Do an experiment to find out what *concave* lenses do to light.
- Design and do an experiment to show that light rays from a distant object are parallel.

EXPERIMENT 5

THE BLIND SPOT

The optic nerve carries nerve impulses from the eye's retina to the brain. The nerve impulses are caused by light striking light receptors (rod and cone cells) in the retina.

THINGS YOU WILL NEED

- **white index card**
- **black felt-tip pen**
- **ruler**

The optic nerve enters the back of the eye and then extends to the brain. (See Figure 3.) At this entry point there are no rod or cone cells. Consequently, you can expect to find a blind spot in every normal eye.

1. You can find the blind spot in your eye. On a white index card, use a black felt-tip pen to draw an **X** and a solid circle. Both figures should be about 5 millimeters (3/8 in) wide. They should be about 7 cm (3 in) apart.

2. Close your right eye and hold the card at arm's length with the circle directly in front of your left eye. Keep your left eye focused on the solid circle as you slowly move the card toward your left eye. You will find a point where the **X** disappears.

3. Turn the card upside down and repeat the experiment with your right eye open and your left eye closed. Explain why the **X** disappears.

CHAPTER TWO

CLASSIFYING THINGS

When you look around, you see a variety of living organisms. Some of them can be grouped based on their similarities. For example, you might classify your dog and cat as domestic animals. Placing objects into groups based on similarities or differences is called classification. Humans like to classify. You probably classify your clothes without much thought. Shirts and pants go in one drawer, sweaters in another, while jackets or dresses are hung in a closet. In dictionaries words are classified alphabetically. Those beginning with the letter "a" precede those beginning with "b."

Part of biology involves classification. Biologists classify organisms, and they often use their system to identify organisms.

BIOLOGICAL CLASSIFICATION

When you observe living organisms, you may notice their differences, but similarities abound as well. A robin is more like a bluebird than a salamander. Both robins and bluebirds have wings and fly, reproduce by laying eggs, and bring food to their young until they can fend for themselves. However, robins and bluebirds differ in color, size, and other features. A robin and a bluebird can't mate and produce offspring.

In general, biologists classify organisms that can mate and reproduce as members of the same species. This classification is not perfect. For example, a horse and a donkey are regarded as separate species because of their differences in size, shape, and general appearance. However, horses and donkeys can mate. A male donkey (jack) and a female horse (mare) can produce offspring that are called mules. Mules, however, are sterile. They cannot reproduce.

The system for classifying living organisms was devised by Carl von Linné (1707–1778). Your first and last name allow others to identify you, Linné's system is similar. It consists of two names for a member of a species. The first, the genus name, is capitalized. It identifies a particular group of organisms that are very similar but do not interbreed. The second is the species name, which is not capitalized. It identifies a group of very similar organisms that can mate and reproduce. For uniformity, Linné chose Latin names. (He even Latinized his own name to Carolus Linnaeus.)

Your species name is *Homo sapiens.* It means "man, wise." Humans are the only living members of the genus *Homo.* However, fossils have been found that are so similar to us they share the genus name. These include *Homo habilis, Homo heidelbergensis, Homo rudolfensis, Homo ergaster, Homo erectus,* and *Homo neanderthalensis.* The oldest of these species lived nearly two million years ago.

Linné recognized nine thousand distinct species. Today more than 1.5 million species have been identified and millions more have yet to be classified.

The biological classification includes more and more species as we ascend the system. Just as similar species are grouped into one genus, so are similar genuses grouped into families. *Homo sapiens* belong to the family Hominidae who all share or shared the ability to walk

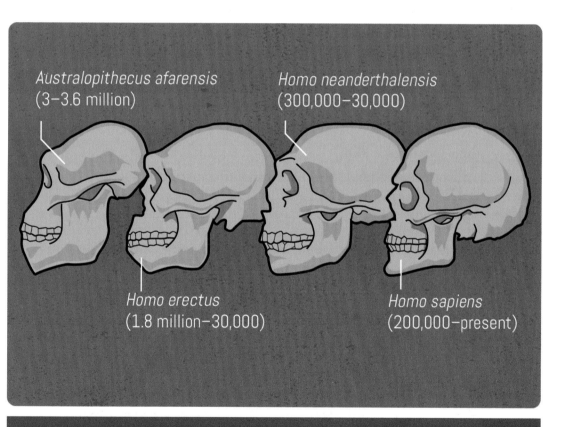

Australopithecus afarensis
(3–3.6 million)

Homo neanderthalensis
(300,000–30,000)

Homo erectus
(1.8 million–30,000)

Homo sapiens
(200,000–present)

Figure 5. These drawings show reconstructions of fossil skulls. The approximate ages of the fossils (years ago) are beneath the species names. Three of the fossils are in the same genus (*Homo*) as humans. *Australopithecus afarensis* was a member of the same family as humans (Hominidae) and walked erect, but differences in bone structure and brain size indicate a different genus.

upright on two feet. Again, we are the only living members of that family. But fossil evidence reveals that some early ancestors, such as *Australopithecus afarensis, Australopithecus boisei, Australopithecus robustus,* and others were members of the same family.

Families are grouped into orders. Humans belong to the order Primates, an order we share with apes (chimpanzees, gorillas, orangutans, and gibbons), monkeys, tree shrews, lemurs, and tarsiers. Primates have both eyes on the front of their head and possess flexible fingers. Some have toes that can grasp objects. The top ends of these fingers and toes are covered by nails, not claws.

Orders are grouped into classes. Humans belong to the class Mammalia. Mammals are born alive and are nursed by their mother's milk.

Mammals all belong to the phylum Vertebrata. Vertebrates have a nerve cord that is enclosed in a series of bones (vertebrae) that make up a backbone. Thus, all classes of animals with a backbone are included in the phylum Vertebrata—bony fish, amphibians, reptiles, and aves (birds), as well as mammals.

Humans belong to the kingdom Animalia (animals), which is part of the domain Eukarya. There are three other kingdoms—protists, fungi, and plants.

Protists are single-celled organisms. Their cells contain a nucleus surrounded by a membrane as well as specialized cell parts (organelles). You may have seen protists such as amoeba and paramecia under a microscope.

Fungi, such as molds and mushrooms, have threadlike cells that attach to and absorb food from other living or dead organisms.

The plant kingdom contains many-celled organisms whose cells have rigid walls made of cellulose. Within their cells is a pigment (chlorophyll) needed for photosynthesis, a process by which plants manufacture their own food by combining carbon dioxide and water using the energy in sunlight.

Members of the Animal kingdom have many cells too, but their cells do not have rigid walls and they cannot make their own food. As a result, most animals have to move about in order to obtain food.

At the top of the classification system biologists have established three domains—Eukarya, Archaea, and Bacteria. Eukarya include the animal, plant, and fungi kingdoms, as well as protists that have cells with nuclei and organelles. Organelles are small structures outside a cell's nucleus where important chemical reactions take place.

Archaea and Bacteria are single-celled organisms. They differ in their genetic structure.

CLASSIFICATION OF SOME ANIMALS

Approximately 97 percent of all known animals are invertebrates—animals without backbones—such as mollusks, worms, insects, and crustaceans. The primary classes of the vertebrate phylum are Osteichthyes (bony fish),

Amphibia (amphibians), Reptilia (reptiles), Aves (birds), and Mammalia (mammals). All the classes are egg-laying, except for most mammals whose embryos grow within their mothers' bodies and are born alive.

Members of the class Osteichthyes live in water. They respire by means of gills and have two-chambered hearts. Amphibians have three-chambered hearts. They are usually aquatic after hatching and respire by means of gills. However, as they mature, they develop lungs, breathe air, and acquire two pairs of legs by which they are able to move on land. Reptiles hatch from eggs that have shells. They have lungs throughout life and possess four-chambered hearts, although the ventricles that pump blood out of the heart are connected by an opening in the wall between the two chambers. Birds have feathers, which are modifications of the scales found on reptiles. Their front appendages are feathered wings that allow many of them to fly. They have lungs for breathing and possess a four-chambered heart without openings between the ventricles. Mammals also have lungs and four-chambered hearts and have hair (modified scales).

One order within the class Mammalia, Monotremata, lays eggs. The best known member of this order is the duck-billed platypus. Another order, Marsupialia, bears live young but transfers them to a pouch where they attach to a nipple and are nourished until they can fend for themselves. Kangaroos, opossums, and koalas are examples of marsupials.

Bats belong to the order Chiroptera. Their forelimbs evolved into wings, enabling them to fly.

Rats, mice, squirrels and similar animals belong to the order Rodentia. They have chisel-like incisor teeth, no canines, and broad molars.

The order Carnivora includes dogs, cats, hyenas, seals, and other animals that have small incisor teeth, large canines, and premolars adapted for shearing meat.

Whales belong to the order Cetacea. Their front limbs have been modified into flippers. They lack rear appendages and are ocean-dwelling throughout their lives. There is good evidence that Cetacea evolved from members of the order Artiodactyla—herbivorous animals with two or four toes modified into hoofs. Artiodactyla include cattle, sheep, pigs, goats, camels, hippopotamuses, and other hoofed mammals.

EXPERIMENT 6

CLASSIFYING ANIMALS

Classifying animals begins at the most general level (domain) and becomes increasingly more specific as you move through kingdom, phylum, class, order, family, genus, and finally species.

1. Prepare a chart similar to the one shown below.
2. The last row of the chart has common names of five common species for you to classify.

3. From what you have read in this book, and from other information you can gather from encyclopedias, the internet, biology textbooks, and books about animals, fill in the chart so as to classify the species whose common names are given. The column for humans has been completed.

THINGS YOU WILL NEED

- **copy of the chart in this experiment**
- **encyclopedias and books about animals**
- **paper**
- **pen or pencil**

Use a copy of this chart to classify species whose common names are given.

DOMAIN	Eukarya				
KINGDOM	Animal				
PHYLUM	Vertebrate				
CLASS	Mammal				
ORDER	Primate				
FAMILY	Hominidae				
GENUS	*Homo*				
SPECIES	*sapiens*				
COMMON NAME	human	cat	dog	horse	mouse

CLASSIFYING PLANTS

The plant kingdom can be divided into flowering and non-flowering plants. Non-flowering plants include mosses, liverworts, ferns, horsetails, and club mosses. These plants reproduce by producing spores. Conifers, which belong to the class Gymnospermae, are trees such as pines. These trees produce seeds, but the seeds develop inside cones, not flowers, and are not surrounded by a fruit.

Flowering plants are in the class Angiospermae. The parts of a typical flower are shown in Figure 6a. Sepals are the outermost parts of a flower. They are often green and leaf-like; however, in some flowers, such as tulips and lilies, the sepals are often the same color as the petals. Sepals protect and cover young flowers before their buds open. Petals are usually the bright, colorful part of a flower that lies just inside, and often between, the sepals. Sepals and petals are called the accessory parts of a flower because they are not directly involved in producing seeds.

The essential parts of the flower—pistils and stamens—are needed to produce seeds. The stamens consist of long slender filaments with little knobs at their ends called anthers. Very fine grains of pollen are found on the anthers. If you rub your finger across an anther, you may be able to see some of the fine yellow dust-like particles of pollen. Perhaps you can collect some pollen and look at it under a microscope.

The pistil or pistils are the female part(s) of a flower. They are usually in the flower's center. The tip of the pistil,

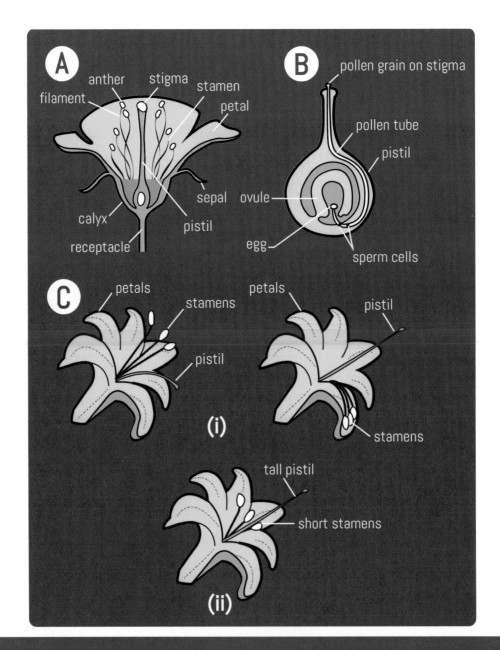

Figure 6. a) This drawing shows the parts of a typical flower. b) A pollen tube grows down the pistil. Sperm cells move along the pollen tube and fertilize the egg or eggs in the ovule at the base of the pistil. c) Two ways to avoid self-pollination include: (i) maturation of stamens and pistils at different times; (ii) tall pistils that tower well above the same flower's stamens.

the stigma, has a sticky substance that helps collect pollen grains carried to the pistil by insects, wind, water, or gravity if the pollen comes from the same flower. A pollen grain produces a long tube through which sperm cells travel to the egg located at the lower end of the pistil, as shown in Figure 6b. The union of sperm and egg produces an embryo that eventually becomes part of the seed. Flowers that receive pollen from another plant of the same species are said to be cross pollinated.

CHAPTER THREE

AN INSIDE LOOK AT PLANTS AND ANIMALS

Dissection is an important part of biology. Although you can learn a lot by observing plants and animals in their natural state, more can be learned by looking inside them. In this chapter you'll look inside a flower and a chicken wing. Then you'll compare the bone structure inside the wing with the bone structure in your arm.

EXPERIMENT 7

A FLOWER TO DISSECT

The best way to see the parts of a flower is to dissect a large one. A daffodil, lily, snapdragon, or tulip would be a good flower to dissect. If you can't find one growing at home, you may be able to obtain wilted ones free at a florist shop if you explain why you need them.

1. Look at the whole flower before you begin dissecting. You can refer to Figure 6.
2. The green cup-like structure that connects the flower to the stem or receptacle is the calyx. The calyx is made up of the sepals. How many sepals are there on the flower you are dissecting? Are they green or another color?
3. The petals make up the colored blossom that most people think of when they hear the word "flower. How many petals does your flower have? Are the petals and sepals equal in number?
4. Use your fingers or tweezers to carefully remove the petals. You should be able to see the stamens and pistil or pistils at the flower's center. How many stamens does your flower have? How many pistils? A magnifying glass may help you to see the parts more clearly. Draw a picture of the flower you have dissected.

EXPERIMENT 8

GERMINATING SEEDS

As a flower dies, the seeds it bears contain the potential for new plants. Germinating seeds reveal the emergence of life from something that was previously dormant and seemingly lifeless. In this experiment you will find what is needed to change an apparently inert seed into a growing seedling.

THINGS YOU WILL NEED

- **4 wide, shallow trays**
- **water**
- **paper towels**
- **seeds–lima bean, navy bean, radish, corn, lentil, peas, and others**
- **plastic wrap**
- **stick-on labels**
- **refrigerator**
- **dark room or closet**

1. Cover the bottoms of four large shallow trays with two or three layers of paper towels. In three of the trays dampen (don't soak) the towels with water.
2. Place about a dozen seeds of each kind you want to germinate in separate regions on the towels in each tray. Then cover the trays with clear plastic wrap. Leave one end of the plastic loose so air can reach the seeds. The clear plastic covers will reduce the rate

at which water evaporates from the towels while still allowing you to observe the seeds.

3. Apply stick-on labels to the plastic wrap so you can identify the seeds in the trays.

4. Place one of the trays with damp towels in a refrigerator.

5. Leave two trays, one with damp towels and one with dry towels, in a warm room.

6. Place another tray with damp towels in a warm, dark room or closet.

7. Check the seeds each day. Add enough water to keep the damp towels moist. Do not add water to the tray with the dry towel.

8. After watching the seeds for a few days, see if you can answer the following questions. Can seeds germinate without being in soil? Is water essential for germination? Is light or darkness essential for seeds to germinate? Is either light or darkness essential for *some kinds* of seeds to germinate? Which seeds germinate quickly? Which seeds take a long time to germinate?

EXPLORING ON YOUR OWN

- Design an experiment to find out whether pea seeds will germinate in colder temperatures than corn seeds.
- Will the birdseed you buy in a store germinate?
- Does temperature affect germination? If it does, how?

EXPERIMENT 9

FOOD IN LEAVES

While flowers make it possible for plants to reproduce, it is their leaves that nourish them and make food for humans as well. Leaves are green because they contain pigments that absorb most of the colors in white light except green. Because light falling on green leaves is reflected instead of being absorbed, most leaves appear green. One of the pigments in the cells of a plant's leaves is chlorophyll.

THINGS YOU WILL NEED

- **an adult**
- **paper clip**
- **black construction paper or aluminum foil**
- **geranium plant**
- **oven mitts**
- **safety glasses**
- **tongs**
- **stove**
- **pan of boiling water**
- **alcohol**
- **small jar**
- **tincture of iodine**

Chlorophyll absorbs light, which provides the energy plants need to carry on photosynthesis. During photosynthesis a plant changes carbon dioxide and water to oxygen and sugar. The oxygen that all living things need to carry on respiration is produced during photosynthesis, which takes place in green plants.

1. Excess sugar produced in a leaf is changed to starch and stored, so you can use the common test for starch (iodine) to confirm that food is produced in leaves when light is present. To carry out this test, begin by using a paper clip to hold a small folded piece of black construction paper or aluminum foil over both sides of a geranium leaf as shown in Figure 7. Be careful not to damage the leaf when you attach the paper. Do this in the morning on a bright sunny day when lots of light will fall on the geranium's leaves.

folded piece of
black paper

paper clip

Figure 7. Use a paper clip to fasten a piece of black construction paper to a geranium leaf. Light will not be able to reach the covered leaf cells, but it will reach the other leaf cells.

2. After four or five hours, pick the leaf from the plant, bring it indoors, and remove the cover.

3. **Under adult supervision**, and while wearing oven mitts and safety glasses, use tongs to hold the leaf's stem. Immerse the rest of the leaf into a pan of boiling water on a stove. Hold the leaf under the boiling water for about one minute. The heat will break open cell walls within the leaf.

4. Next, use alcohol to extract the green chlorophyll from the leaf. To do this, first **turn off the stove** because **alcohol is flammable** and should never be brought near a flame or red hot burner.

5. Place the now limp leaf in a jar of alcohol and leave it overnight.

6. The next morning you will find the alcohol has a green color due to the pigments it has extracted from the leaf. (If the leaf is still greenish, leave it in the alcohol longer.) Put your safety glasses on again. Mix together in a saucer approximately equal amounts of tincture of iodine solution and water, about 5 mL of each will do. **Remember: Iodine is poisonous. Handle it carefully!**

7. Next, rinse the leaf in warm water before you spread it out and place it in the iodine-water solution.

    You will see the leaf turn color as the iodine reacts with the starch to form a dark blue-black color. Notice that one area of the leaf is much lighter than the rest. Can you identify that region?

In which area of the leaf did photosynthesis not take place? How can you tell? What evidence do you have to show that light is required for photosynthesis?

EXPERIMENT

PLANTS AND CARBON DIOXIDE

During photosynthesis plants combine carbon dioxide and water in the presence of light to produce food and oxygen. The food is either stored by the plant or used as an energy source. (Plants, like you, use food for energy.) The process by which energy is obtained from food is called respiration. During respiration, food is oxidized; that is, the food combines with oxygen in a complicated series of chemical reactions. The end products of respiration are

THINGS YOU WILL NEED

- **4 test tubes**
- **water**
- **masking tape**
- **marking pen**
- **bromthymol blue solution (perhaps your school's science department will let you borrow some)**
- **dropper with mL marks**
- **drinking straw**
- **sprigs of the water plant elodea**
- **4 rubber stoppers or corks that fit test tubes**
- **4 glasses or beakers**
- **light bulb**
- **dark room or closet**

carbon dioxide and water, the very same chemicals that are combined to make food during photosynthesis. But only green plants can manufacture food, and they can do so only in the presence of light.

1. With the information from the previous paragraph in mind, fill four test tubes about halfway with water. Place a small piece of masking tape on each tube. Label them 1, 2, 3, and 4. Place each tube in a glass or beaker for support.

2. Add 1.0 mL of bromthymol blue to each tube. Bromthymol blue is an acid-base indicator. It is blue in a base, such as ammonia, and yellow in an acid, such as vinegar or a solution of carbon dioxide. Carbon dioxide forms carbonic acid when it dissolves in water.

3. Using a drinking straw, gently blow air from your lungs into tubes 1 and 2. Continue to blow in lung air until no further change occurs. How can you explain the fact that the solutions turn from blue to yellow?

4. Place sprigs of elodea in tubes 1 and 3. (Elodea is a water plant commonly found in ponds or in stores that sell aquarium supplies.)

5. Seal the openings of all four test tubes with rubber stoppers or corks. Place the tubes in glasses or beakers of water near a bright light source. Be sure the tubes are not so close to the light that the water becomes hot.

6. After several hours, record any changes you see. Continue to watch the tubes for an entire day. What changes occur?

What is the purpose of each of the four tubes in this investigation? What do the changes in each tube indicate?

What do you think will happen in each test tube if the tubes are placed in darkness instead of in light?

7. Test your predictions by repeating the experiment with the plants in darkness.

EXPERIMENT 11

FEELING BENEATH THE SKIN

Before you go beneath the skin in the next experiment, feel the bone structure under the skin of your arm or a friend's arm.

THINGS YOU WILL NEED

- **your arm or the arm of a friend**

1. Begin at the upper arm. The rounded upper end of the humerus (the upper arm bone) fits into and can rotate in the glenoid cavity of the shoulder. You won't be able to feel this because it's under muscle tissue. However,

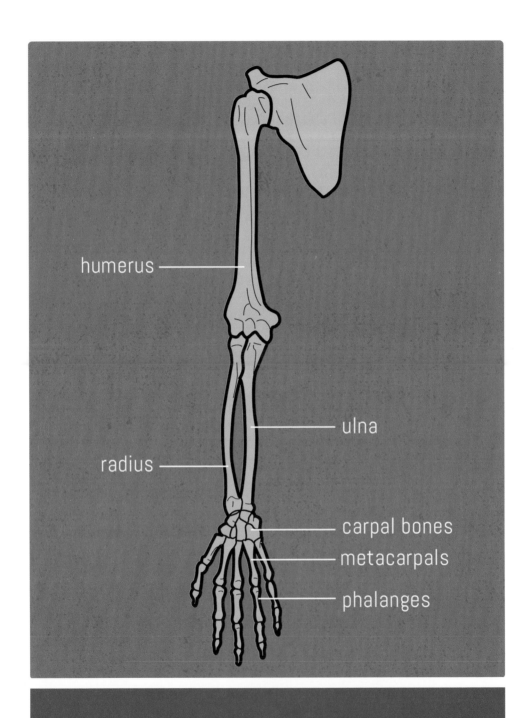

Figure 8. The bones in a human arm

you can feel the shaft of your or a friend's humerus at the center of your upper arm. Refer to Figure 8.

2. You will find that the lower end of the humerus is wide and articulates with the two bones of the lower arm.

3. What we call the elbow is the upper end of the ulna. If you follow the ulna downward, you will find that it ends in the knob-like styloid process above the little-finger side of the wrist.

4. The styloid process of the other bone of the lower arm—the radius—can be found above the thumb-side of the wrist. You can follow the radius upward to the point where it articulates with the humerus.

5. The wrist is made up of eight small bones called the carpals, which are difficult to identify individually. You can, however, feel the five metacarpal bones on the back of your hand.

6. The lower ends of these bones articulate with the phalanges, or fingers. There are a total of fourteen phalanges on each hand. Three are found in each finger and two in the thumb. The joints where meta-carpals and phalanges meet are commonly known as your knuckles.

As you can see from Figure 9, many mammals have the same "arm" bones even though their relative sizes vary greatly. Such structures are said to be homologous because the bones have the same origin and basic structure even though they serve different purposes. Similarly, as Figure 10 reveals, the hand bones are also homologous.

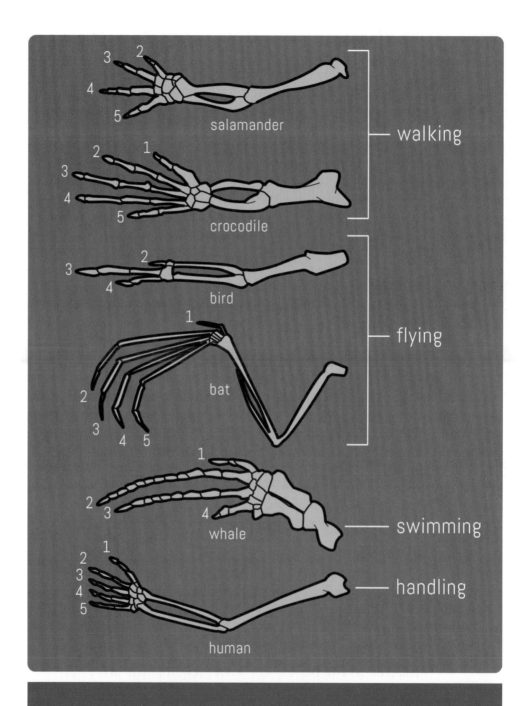

Figure 9. These forelimbs are homologous. What differences do you see? What do the numbers indicate?

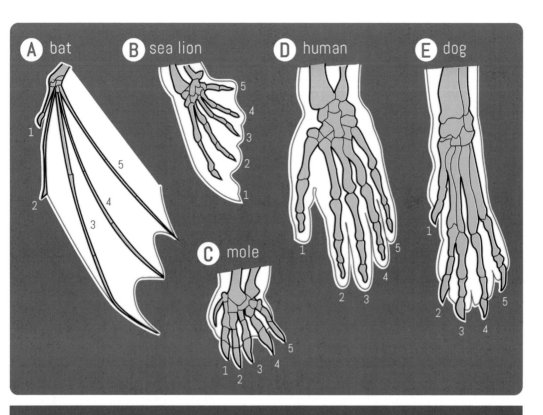

Figure 10. All these mammals have the same "hand" bones, but in different proportions. a) a bat's wing; b) a sea lion's flipper; c) a mole's paw; d) a human hand; e) a dog's paw.

Even the embryonic development of vertebrates is very similar as shown in Figure 11.

The leg bones are similar in some ways to those of the arm. The upper leg has a single bone, the femur. The femur is the longest bone in your body. The rounded head at its upper end fits into a concavity in the side of the pelvis. The lower leg, like the arm, has two bones, the tibia and the fibula.

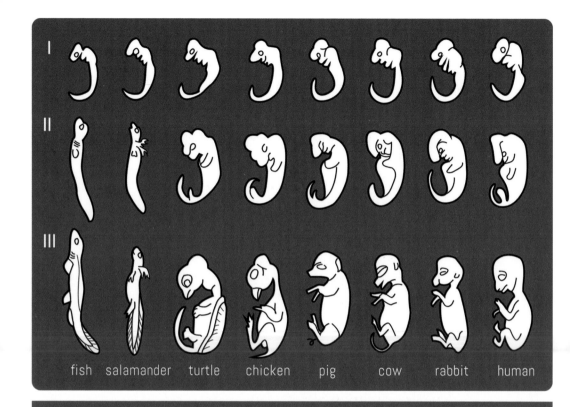

fish   salamander   turtle   chicken   pig   cow   rabbit   human

Figure 11. The vertebrate embryos in the top row are seen a few days after fertilization of an egg by a sperm. Notice their similarities despite the fact that they develop into a range of vertebrates from fish to humans. Embryos in the middle row are a few days older and are more distinct. Embryos in the third row are still older. They have developed to a stage that allows you to see what species they will be at birth or hatching.

7. You can feel the outer upper end of the femur move as you walk.

8. Feel the very wide lower end of your femur. It lies behind your patella (knee cap). The upper part of the femur is buried in muscles and probably can't be felt.

9. The lower end of the femur articulates with the tibia (shin bone). It is the larger of the two bones of the lower leg. You can feel the entire front side of the tibia. Start just below the patella and follow it to its bulb-like end on the inner (medial) side of your leg at the ankle.

10. The bulb-like end of the tibia, the medial malleolus, has its complement on the other side of the ankle— the lateral malleolus.

11. The lateral malleolus is the lower end of the fibula, which lies on the outer (lateral) side of your leg. How far can you trace the fibula up your leg?

12. Like the wrist, the ankle consists of a number of bones (7)—the tarsals. The largest tarsal bone is the heel bone or calcaneus, which you can feel on the lower rear portion of your foot.

    The metatarsals lie between the toes and the ankle and correspond to the metacarpal bones in the hand. You can probably feel all five of your metatarsals by moving your fingers over the top of your foot behind your toes.

13. The front ends of the metatarsals articulate with the phalanges, commonly known as toes. Your toes, like your fingers, have a total of fourteen phalanges on each foot. There are three phalanges in each of the four smaller toes and two in the great (big) toe.

EXPLORING ON YOUR OWN

- On a real or plastic model of a human skeleton, or on detailed anatomical diagrams, how many bones can you identify? (See Figure 12.)

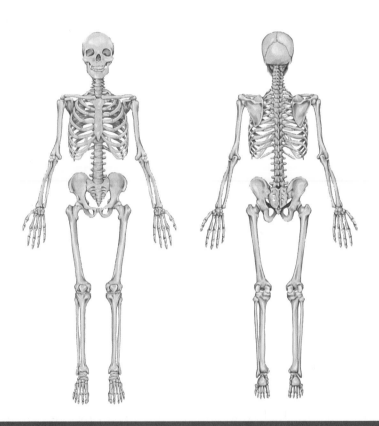

Figure 12. Front and rear view of a human skeleton

- What is the meaning of the words "axial" and "appendicular" as they apply to your skeleton?
- Why do police often ask anthropologists to examine skeletons at crime scenes? How do anthropologists distinguish between male and female skeletons?
- Visit a science museum where the skeletons of different animals are on display. Can you identify bones in these animals that are similar to those found in humans?

EXPERIMENT

SEEING WHAT'S UNDER THE SKIN

There are bones, muscles, tendons, and ligaments inside animal bodies including your own. But you have to go under the skin to see them. In this experiment you will actually see them by looking beneath the skin of an uncooked chicken wing.

1. Put the chicken wing on a thick layer of newspapers. **Ask an adult to help you cut it apart** so you can see the different tissues for yourself. The adult will need a sharp knife, and you'll need a pair of tweezers, scissors, and a probe to pull and cut tissues, as well as paper towels to wipe your hands.

2. Most of the skin covering the wing can be pulled away with your fingers. As you pull it off, look for connective tissue that attaches the skin to the muscles underneath.

3. The flesh beneath the skin and fatty tissue is mostly muscle. Notice how each muscle is covered by a very thin transparent membrane.

THINGS YOU WILL NEED

- **an adult**
- **chicken wing**
- **newspapers**
- **sharp knife**
- **tweezers**
- **finishing nail or small metal rod**
- **scissors**
- **probe such as a slender stick or finishing nail**
- **paper towels**
- **garbage container**
- **soap and water**

4. Use tweezers and a probe, such as a finishing nail or small metal rod, to separate the muscles from one another. See if you can find the origin and insertion onto the bone of several muscles.

5. Find the tough, white, fibrous tendons that connect the muscles to bone. Use scissors to cut the tendons and remove the muscles to expose the bones.

6. The major bones in the wing are very similar to the arm bones you examined in Experiment 11. Can you find the humerus? Can you find the radius and ulna?

How do the carpals, metacarpals, and phalanges of a chicken differ from yours?

7. Find the wide, tough, white ligaments that connect the humerus to the radius and ulna bones. Use scissors to cut through the ligaments that join these bones.

8. Examine the ends of the bones. Can you find glistening white cartilage covering them? What do you think is the function of this cartilage? Can you find pads of yellow fat within the joint?

9. **Ask the adult** to cut away the tissue along the bones.

10. Place the tissue in a garbage container.

11. **Wash your hands thoroughly with soap and water when you have finished handling the chicken wing.**

CHAPTER FOUR

DARWIN AND THE THEORY OF EVOLUTION

You may hear someone refer to evolution as "just a theory." But what is a scientific theory? In ordinary conversation, someone might say, "I have a theory about that," meaning a guess or a hunch. In science, a theory is much more. It is a well developed explanation of some aspect of the natural world that is supported by *a lot* of evidence. During the early 1500s, Copernicus developed the heliocentric theory. It held that Earth and all the other planets orbit the sun. At that time, most people believed the sun, stars, and other planets revolved about the earth. Gradually, the heliocentric theory became accepted because it provided a better explanation of what astronomers observed than did the geocentric (earth-centered) theory. Similarly, the atomic theory, which assumes that matter is made of atoms, is accepted by scientists. It can explain the observations and experimental evidence that have been gathered about the behavior and structure of matter.

The theory of evolution is widely accepted by scientists because it offers the best explanation of what is known about biology and geology. In fact, biology would be a very puzzling subject without the theory of evolution.

CHARLES DARWIN AND THE THEORY OF EVOLUTION

At age twenty-two, Charles Darwin was floundering. He had studied medicine and theology but had no interest in either. But, in 1831, despite his father's disapproval, he joined the crew of the *Beagle* as an unpaid naturalist on a five-year journey. Four years later, the *Beagle* anchored off the Galapagos Islands about 1,000 kilometers (600 miles) west of South America.

Darwin spent nearly a month there observing and collecting plants and animals. He was particularly impressed by the giant tortoises, mockingbirds, and finches. The finches resembled those he had seen in Ecuador, but they were much more diverse. While finches normally eat seeds, some were eating fleshy cacti, others worms, some fed on insects, and others on fruits. One species, the woodpecker finch, used the spine from a cactus to pry under tree bark to drive out insects. Such a niche would normally be occupied by woodpeckers, but there were none on the Galapagos. A species of finch had taken advantage of that food source. There were finches everywhere, some big, some small, some in trees, and some on the ground. Interestingly, the different species had different beaks, beaks that were adapted to the kind of food they ate (see Figure 13).

Figure 13. Darwin was struck by the differences in the beaks of the various species of finches he observed on the Galapagos Islands.

At that time, most people believed God had created every species as stated in the Book of Genesis. But Darwin, reflecting on what he had seen, had a different explanation. He believed a few finches had been carried by winds to the Galapagos Islands. Once there, birds on each island had slowly adapted to survive on the food available to them. Birds with variations best suited for survival on available food became different from their ancestors. They might, for example, become larger or stronger. Eventually, over many generations, they became distinct species.

DARWIN AND THE BEAKS OF FINCHES

While on the Galapagos Islands, Darwin observed several species of finches that had never been seen before. He noticed that the beaks of each species had become modified in order to feed on specific foods.

In this experiment a plastic spoon, knife, and fork, as well as pliers with different ends (needle nose, adjustable, and regular), will represent different beaks. The "beaks" will be used to "eat" a variety of seeds.

THINGS YOU WILL NEED

- **plastic spoon, knife, and fork**
- **pliers with different ends (needle nose, adjustable, and regular)**
- **seeds of at least 6 kinds such as thistle, sunflower, radish, carrot, lettuce, squash, and corn**
- **teaspoon**
- **tablespoon**
- **paper plates**
- **clock or stopwatch**
- **a partner**
- **notebook**
- **pen or pencil**
- **graph paper**

1. Place a teaspoonful of each of the smaller seeds and a tablespoonful of the larger seeds on a paper plate.

2. Ask a partner to use one of the "beaks" to "eat" seeds for one minute. Put each seed "eaten" on a second paper plate.
3. After one minute, count and record the number of seeds of each type that are on the second plate.
4. Place the seeds that were "eaten" back on the first plate. Have your partner repeat the experiment for each of the other "beaks."
5. After all the "beaks" have been tested, plot bar graphs such as the one in Figure 14 for each beak that was tested.

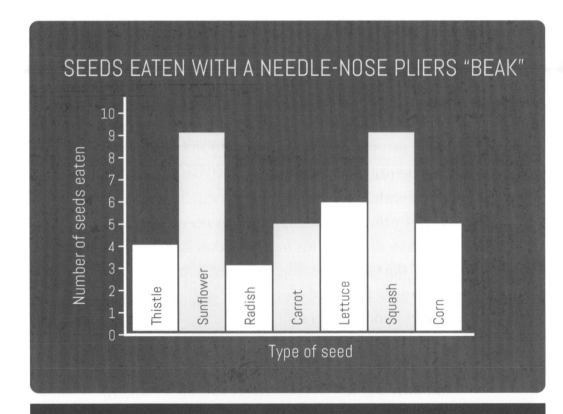

Figure 14. A bar graph of the seeds "eaten" by a particular beak. Your results may be quite different.

Which beak or beaks seemed best adapted for eating a particular seed?

Which beak seemed best adapted for eating a variety of seeds?

Were any beaks limited to eating only one kind of seed? If that seed were to become extinct, what would happen to that species?

Which beak seemed best adapted for survival?

EXPERIMENT 14

SEEDS ACROSS A SEA

Darwin found plants on the Galapagos Islands that he had seen in South America. He reasoned that seeds had been carried by the wind or floated across ocean waters on driftwood or on their own from island to island until they reached the Galapagos. But could seeds survive in the ocean's salt water? He tested his hypothesis by doing experiments similar to one you can do.

1. The primary salt dissolved in sea water is sodium chloride, the salt you put on food. The salt concentration in oceans is 3.5 percent. If you live near the ocean, collect some sea water and bring it home. If

THINGS YOU'LL NEED:

- **sea water or a salt solution**
- **teaspoon**
- **kosher salt**
- **graduated cylinder or metric measuring cup**
- **water**
- **bowl**
- **plastic wrap**
- **marking pen**
- **various kinds of seeds—radish, peas, cucumbers, beans, asparagus, squash, corn**
- **Styrofoam cups**
- **garden or potting soil**
- **large aluminum pan**

    you don't live near an ocean, you can make some sea water.

2. Add about 3.5 g (a teaspoonful) of kosher salt to 100 mL (3.4 oz) of water and stir until the salt dissolves.

3. Pour the salt water into a bowl. Cover the bowl loosely with plastic wrap to reduce evaporation.

4. Add four or five seeds of each kind to the salt water. Be sure you can recognize each seed by its size and shape. Some seeds will sink; others will float.

5. Leave the seeds in the water for twenty-four hours. While the seeds are soaking, fill Styrofoam cups with moist soil.

6. Place the cups on a large aluminum pan. There should be as many cups as there are types of seed.

7. After twenty-four hours, plant the seeds about 0.5 cm (0.25 in) deep in the soil. Plant only one kind of seed in a cup. Use a marking pen to label the cups with the name of the seed planted.

8. Keep the soil moist but not soggy. It may take anywhere from two days to two weeks for seeds to germinate. Did any of the seeds germinate? If so, which ones were they?

9. Repeat the experiment, but this time leave the seeds in the salt water for forty-eight hours. Can any of the seeds sprout after forty-eight hours in salt water? Can any germinate after being in salt water for three days? Can any survive a week in ocean water?

   Darwin found that some seeds can germinate after a long time in ocean water. What did you find?

THE FOSSIL RECORD AND EVOLUTION

During the *Beagle*'s voyage, Darwin read Charles Lyell's book, *Principles of Geology*. It convinced him that Earth had undergone major changes over long periods of time. If rocks can change with time, he thought, perhaps living things can also change. In fact, he knew that domesticated animals, such as dogs, chickens, pigeons, horses, and cattle, had been deliberately changed. Breeders had selected traits they wanted to transmit to succeeding generations. They did this by breeding those animals that possessed the traits they sought, such as speed in horses, herding instincts in dogs, or milk production in cows.

Fossils found in ancient rocks revealed that many plants and animals had become extinct and the older the rocks, the more primitive the fossils. Fossils of mammals were found only in more recent sediments. There seemed to be a progression of species through time. Simple organisms appear in the fossil record before more complex ones. Invertebrates precede vertebrates; fish appear before amphibians; amphibians before reptiles; reptiles before birds; and birds prior to mammals. In addition, as Figure 11 reveals, the embryos of all animals seem very similar in their early stages of development, suggesting they may have had a common ancestor. Further, the anatomy of vertebrates shows a gradual progression from fish to mammals. And the skeletons of mammals as different as whales, bats, and humans are similar but adapted for life in different environments. The evidence convinced Darwin that all life had descended over eons of time from a common ancestor.

It later led him to write *On the Origin of Species,* a book that explained his theory of evolution. He had come to realize that variation among members of a species determines who will succeed in the struggle for survival. Those organisms best adapted (suited) to a particular niche would survive in the competition for the limited food resources. And those organisms would pass on the traits that enabled them to survive to succeeding generations.

Darwin could now explain the variety of finches he had observed on the Galapagos. The first finches to reach the islands would have reproduced until the food supply became limited. But some birds, as a result of their variations, were able to feed on different seeds or a new food source such as the fleshy tissue of a cactus or a fruit. These few birds were able to adapt to a different diet, one that most members of the species could not eat. Birds with the right variations found an untapped niche of the environment and multiplied. Eventually, they changed enough so that they could not interbreed with their ancestors and became a separate species.

NATURAL SELECTION

It was the variations among the members of a species that allowed nature to select those organisms that would survive, those who could take advantage of the opportunities a particular environment offered. He called the process "natural selection" to distinguish it from the artificial selection practiced by breeders of domestic animals and plants. Natural selection, Darwin maintained, was a never-ending process in which organisms better adapted to an environment gradually replaced those that were not as well adapted for survival. Others called it "survival of the fittest." Normal variation coupled with natural selection could explain the process of evolution by which new species appeared through time as others became extinct.

Evolution is usually slow, but examination of the fossil records provides evidence of change. Sometimes the process can be observed within a lifetime. The peppered moth found in England is an example. One variation among peppered moth is their color; some are light, some are dark. At the beginning of the nineteenth century, light-colored moths were far more common than dark ones. By the twentieth century, the reverse was true, but only in urban environments. The ratio in rural regions remained the same. Why?

Biologists offered a hypothesis. The soot from the factories that arose during the industrial revolution had blackened the bark on the trunks of trees where these moths normally stopped to rest. It had also killed the white lichen that grew there. As a result, the lighter moths had become more visible to predators while the darker moths blended into the dark background of the tree trunks.

To test their hypothesis, they placed light- and dark-colored moths on the trunks of trees in rural and in urban areas near factories. At urban sites, more of the light-colored moths were devoured by birds. In rural areas where tree trunks and lichen remained undarkened by soot, the dark-colored moths were the ones more frequently eaten. The experimental test of the hypothesis showed that natural selection favored dark moths in urban areas and lighter moths in rural areas.

By the middle of the twentieth century, the English Parliament passed air pollution laws that greatly reduced the soot from factories. By the end of the century, new trees with light-colored bark housing white lichen had reappeared in cities. And, sure enough, the light-colored moth population increased in urban areas and the number of darker moths declined. The moth population evolved back to the way it was two centuries before.

HOMOLOGOUS ORGANS

One example of evidence for descent from a common ancestor is the existence of homologous organs or body parts. These are parts of the anatomy that form in the same way from the same tissue in embryos. Although the parts are homologous, they may serve very different functions.

You have seen homologous anatomy in Figures 9 and 10. And, in Experiment 12, you saw that the arm of a human and the wing of a chicken contain the same bones. Figures 9 and 10 revealed that homologous bone structure is common in the animal kingdom.

Examine the "hand" bones of different mammals shown in Figure 10. Through evolution these hands, paws, wings, and flippers have taken on different functions. But notice how similar the homologous bones of these mammals are.

The anatomy and embryology of animals, fossils, and extinct animals seemingly ancestral to present-day animals, together with his observations during his voyage on the *Beagle,* came together in Darwin's mind. It convinced him that all living things are related and share a common origin.

NATURAL SELECTION AND SURVIVAL BY COLOR

In this experiment you will simulate natural selection.

THINGS YOU WILL NEED

- **sheets of green, white, black, red, blue, and yellow construction paper**
- **paper punch**
- **friend, sibling, or parent**
- **forceps**
- **sheet of glossy paper**
- **clock or watch**

1. Obtain sheets of green, white, black, red, blue, and yellow construction paper.
2. Use a paper punch to prepare thirty small circular discs from each of the six sheets of paper.
3. Place a sheet of green construction paper on a table. Spread the 180 circles in a random fashion all over the sheet of green paper.
4. Tell a friend, sibling, or parent to pretend to be a "predator," a bird perhaps, that feeds on insects on a green "lawn." The "predator" is to consider the circles as prey representing different varieties of an insect.

5. Hand the "predator" a pair of forceps and tell her to "feed" on the prey. Tell her to pretend to "fly" in random fashion all over the "lawn" and "feed" on the prey.

6. Each "insect" "eaten" is to be dropped on a sheet of glossy paper next to the "lawn."

7. After two or three minutes, ask the "predator" to assume that he or she is sated (full) and return the forceps to you.

8. Use the forceps to separate the circles by color into six separate groups. Then count the number of each color that the predator consumed. What was the color of the "insect" most often "eaten"? Which color was "eaten" least often? Which "insect" seemed best suited for survival? How was it adapted for survival?

EXPERIMENT 16

VARIATION IN HUMANS

There are many variations in living things other than color. You don't have to look far to find them. The hands, tongues, and ears of a

THINGS YOU WILL NEED

- **notebook and pen or pencil**
- **human subjects**

number of humans illustrate variation. Four such variations can be seen in Figure 15.

1. Look at the fingers of different people. Some have index fingers as long as their ring fingers. In others, the index finger is shorter than the ring finger. Some people have curved thumbs; others have straight thumbs. There are people who can roll their tongues, but many cannot. The earlobes of people may be attached or free.

2. With their permission, examine a number of people for the traits shown in Figure 15. What percentage of the people you observed had index and ring fingers that were approximately equal in length? What percentage did not? How about curved and straight thumbs? How many could roll their tongues? How about earlobes? What percentage were attached?

   Do any of these traits provide an advantage to those who possess them?

3. Can you wiggle your ears? Some people have the muscles needed to do this. What percentage of people have these muscles?

4. Name some animals that can move their ears. Is it advantageous for an animal to move its ears? How about humans? Why do you think some people have the muscles that allow them to move their ears?

EXPLORING ON YOUR OWN

- What other variable human traits can you examine? Which are rare? Do any provide an evolutionary advantage?
- At a zoo or farm, examine as many members of a single animal species as possible. What variations do you notice among these animals? How are they suited for the environment they normally inhabit?

LAMARCK'S THEORY

Charles Darwin was not the first to observe that organisms change over time. In 1809, Jean Lamarck (1744–1829) proposed that living organisms acquire traits that help them adapt to their environment. Once acquired, he said, the

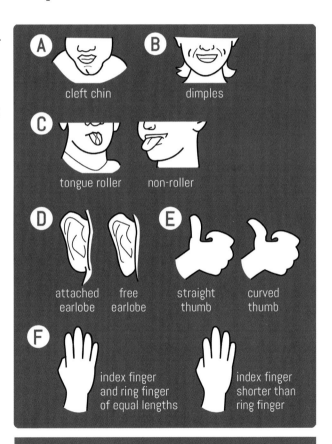

Figure 15. A few of the many variations in humans can be found in their: a) chins; b dimples; c) tongues; d) earlobes; e) thumbs; and f) index and ring fingers.

traits are passed on to offspring. Over time a species could evolve into a form very different from its ancestors. As an example, Lamarck explained the giraffe's long neck. It was acquired, he argued, because as these animals stretched their necks to reach leaves near the tops of trees, their necks became longer. Once they possessed longer necks, the trait was transmitted to their offspring. Gradually, over centuries, the giraffes acquired their long necks.

According to Darwin, both longer- and shorter-necked giraffes existed. In the struggle for survival, those with longer necks had an advantage that made them more likely to obtain food and thus produce offspring that would have long necks. Over time, animals with longer necks replaced those with shorter necks.

Lamarck's theory was discredited by a variety of experiments. In one experiment, August Weismann (1834–1914) cut off the tails of more than fifteen hundred mice over a span of twenty-two generations. In every generation, the mice were still born with tails.

Darwin summarized his theory of evolution as "descent with modification." Variations in a species make some better adapted for survival than others. The better adapted are more likely to live, reproduce, and transmit their traits to the next generation. Over time, the better adapted organisms become the predominant form of the species or become a new species.

CHAPTER FIVE

FROM DARWIN TO MENDEL: THE EXPLANATION FOR VARIATION

Darwin knew that evolution depended on the variations among members of a species. However, he could not explain why variations occur. His critics attacked him on this weak point in his theory. At that time, people believed inherited traits blended, that offspring were a melding of their parents' traits. Consequently, critics argued, any variation providing an advantage in the struggle for survival would soon disappear. The variation would be diluted when blended with traits of the variant's mate. Their offspring's traits would be blended further by mating with ordinary individuals.

Gregor Mendel (1822–1884), an Austrian monk, did experiments to find out how living things come to differ. His work is the foundation of genetics. He discovered why variations in a species persist. They do not blend; a variation can be transmitted through many generations.

Mendel began growing pea plants in his monastery's garden in 1857, two years before Darwin published *On the Origin of Species*. However, Mendel's work went unnoticed until it was discovered by Hugo de Vries in 1900.

Early in the twentieth century scientists realized that genes, located on chromosomes, control the traits of an organism, but the chemistry of genes and the way they function were not discovered until the second half of the century.

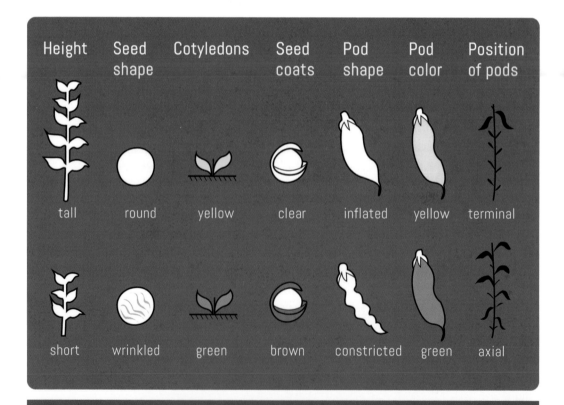

Figure 16. These are the seven traits that vary in the pea plants studied by Gregor Mendel.

Mendel experimented with seven traits in pea plants: height, seed shape, color of the seed leaves (cotyledons), seed coats, pod shape, pod color, and position of pods on the stem. (See Figure 16.)

Mendel started with true-breeding varieties—plants that for many generations showed only one of the two forms for any of the seven traits he studied. He crossed (mated) true-breeding plants with contrasting traits. (These plants were known as the parent or P_1 generation.) To make these crosses, he removed the stamens from, say, the flowers of a tall plant and placed their pollen on the pistils of a short plant. He also removed the stamens from the flowers of short plants and placed their pollen grains on the pistils of tall plants. This prevented the plants from self-pollinating, the way pea plants normally reproduce. He then covered the flowers to prevent pollination by wind or insects.

The seeds produced by the flowers from the P_1 generation were planted and observed. The plants that grew from these seeds, known as the first filial, or F_1 generation, flowered and were allowed to self-pollinate. The seeds produced by the F_1 generation grew into the plants of the second filial, or F_2, generation.

GREGOR MENDEL'S INITIAL EXPERIMENTS

When true-breeding tall plants were crossed with true-breeding short plants in the P_1 generation, all the F_1 plants that grew from their seeds were tall. There were no short plants. So much for the blending theory of inheritance!

However, the factor for shortness had not disappeared. When the F_1 plants self-pollinated to produce the F_2 generation, the results were striking. Both tall and short plants grew from these seeds. The factor for shortness, hidden in the F_1 generation, reappeared in one-fourth of the F_2 plants. The other three-fourths were tall. The ratio of tall to short was 3:1.

When the F_2 generation plants reproduced by self-pollination, Mendel found that all the short plants were true-breeding. They produced only short offspring. One-third of the tall plants were true-breeding; they produced only tall offspring. The other two-thirds produced both tall and short plants in the same ratio (3:1) as their F_1 ancestors. Table 1 summarizes Mendel's results.

Table 1: Mendel's results when crossing true-breeding tall pea plants with true-breeding short pea plants (P_1 generation). An x is used to indicate a cross (mating) between plants with a contrasting trait such as height (tall or short).

Generation	Cross	Ratio of offspring from seeds
P_1	tall x short	F_1: all tall
F_1	tall x tall	F_2: 3 tall:1 short
F_2	short x short	F_3: all short
	1/3 Tall x tall	F_3: all tall
	2/3 Tall x tall	F_3: 3 tall:1 short

Mendel found similar results when he crossed plants for each of the other six contrasting traits. His results for the F_1 and F_2 generations for each of the seven traits he studied are shown in Table 2. In all cases, the F_2 plants produced the same 3:1 pattern of offspring.

The results show that in the F_2 generation one trait is three times as likely to appear as the other. The trait that appears three times as frequently is the same one that appears in all plants in the F_1 generation. Mendel referred to the trait that appeared more frequently in the F_2 generation as a dominant trait. A trait that disappeared in the F_1 generation, such as shortness, he called a recessive trait. When both traits were present in a seed, only the dominant one was seen. Thus, in pea plants, tallness is a dominant trait,

Table 2: Results for Mendel's investigation of seven traits inherited by pea plants in the F_1 and F_2 generations.

P_1 cross	F_1 plants	F_2 plants	Ratio
tall x short	all tall	787 tall 277 short	2.84:1
round x wrinkled seeds	all round	5474 round 1850 wrinkled	2.96:1
yellow x green cotyledons	all yellow	6022 yellow 2001 green	3.01:1
brown x clear seed coats	all brown	705 brown 224 clear	3.15:1
inflated x constricted pods	all inflated	882 inflated 299 constricted	2.95:1
green x yellow pods	all green	428 green 152 yellow	2.82:1
axial x terminal pods	all axial	651 axial 207 terminal	3.14:1

while shortness is a recessive trait. From Table 2, can you identify the dominant and recessive trait in each of the other six characteristics Mendel investigated?

A MODEL TO EXPLAIN MENDEL'S INITIAL EXPERIMENTS

To do Mendel's experiments would take several years so we'll use a model as a way to represent his work with pea plants.

Without reading any further, see if you can develop a model (theory) to explain the results of Mendel's experiments. Then compare your model with his.

THINGS YOU WILL NEED

- **24 dry, dark-colored and 24 dry, light-colored bean seeds similar in size and shape**
- **2 paper cups**
- **notebook and pen or pencil**

Now compare your model with Mendel's. He reasonably assumed that hereditary factors are passed to the next generation through the plants' gametes, which are the sperm cells in the pollen and the egg cells in the pistil.

1. Use the dark beans to represent the factor for tall pea plants. Use light-colored beans to represent the factor for short pea plants. Place two dozen dark beans in one paper cup. This cup represents the tall pea plants. Place an equal number of light-colored beans in a second cup. This cup represents the short pea plants.

2. Inherited factors come from both parents, so let's assume, as Mendel did, that in the P_1 generation the pure-bred tall plants have only the factor for tallness represented by the dark beans. Pure-bred short plants have only the factor for shortness represented by the light-colored beans. Let's assume also, as Mendel did, that the F_1 generation receives only one factor for height from each parent (Figures 17a and 17b).

3. In your model this can be done by taking one bean from each of the two cups and putting them together. Another way is to make a Punnett square (devised by Reginald Punnett, an English geneticist) and let letters (T for tall, t for short) represent the inherited factors. Figure 17c shows how to make a Punnett square for the P_1 and the F_1 crosses where tallness is involved.

   The symbols representing the inherited factors for one parent are listed along the side of the square. The symbols representing the inherited factors for the other parent are listed along the top. Each possible combination of inherited factors that can be found in the offspring is listed inside the square. By counting the number of times a combination appears in

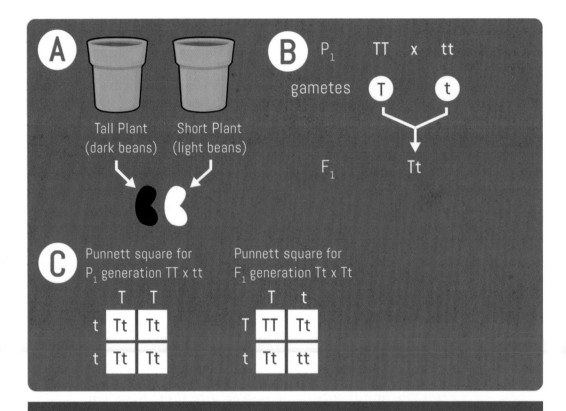

Figure 17. a) Pure-breeding pea plants have only the factor for tallness represented by the dark beans. Pure-breeding short plants have only the factor for shortness, represented here by light-colored beans. The F_1 generation receives one factor for height from each parent. All F_1 plants will be tall because tallness is the dominant factor. b) The cross between tall and short plants can also be represented by symbols, *T* for tall and *t* for short. Gametes from tall plants all carry the factor *T*. Gametes from the short plants all carry the factor *t*. Cells of the F_1 plants have both factors, *T* and *t*, but they are tall because *T* is dominant to *t*. c) The diagrams show Punnett squares for the P_1 and F_1 generations.

the square you can predict the likelihood of that trait appearing in the offspring.

4. As you can see from Figure 17a, Figure 17b, and the first Punnett square in Figure 17c, all the F_1 offspring

will be tall. The factor for tallness, represented by the dark bean or the capital letter T, is dominant to the factor for shortness, represented by the light-colored bean or the small letter t. When the hereditary factors for both tall and short plants are present in a plant's cells, the plant will be tall.

What hereditary factors for height will be in the gametes produced by plants of the F_1 generation? What kind of offspring will be produced?

5. The second Punnett square shows that the inherited factors, T and t, can combine in three different ways: TT, Tt, and tt. Since T is dominant to t, three of every four F_1 offspring can be expected be tall (TT, Tt, and Tt) and one (tt) will be short.

6. To see how this works in a more concrete way, place twenty-four dark beans and twenty-four light-colored beans in the same cup. Cover the cup with your hand and shake it to thoroughly mix the beans. Do the same with a second paper cup. Each cup contains the hereditary factors for height that can be in a gamete produced by an F_1 pea plant. Each cup represents a parent plant from the F_1 generation. Each bean represents a hereditary factor that can be found in a sperm or egg cell (the gametes).

7. Close your eyes and remove a bean (representing a factor for height) from one cup. This bean is the hereditary factor that will be in the sperm. Repeat the procedure for the other cup. This is the hereditary factor that will be in the egg. The two beans

together represent the hereditary factors that will be in the seed.

8. Record the result in your notebook. If you drew two dark beans, record it as *TT* because the factors for height from both parents were for tallness. (The capital *T* shows that it is a dominant factor.) If you drew two light-colored beans, record it as *tt*. (The small letter *t* shows that it is a recessive factor.) If you drew a dark bean and a light-colored bean, record it as *Tt*. (This seed will produce a tall plant, but it also carries the factor for shortness.)

9. Return the beans to their respective cups. Shake the cups again. Repeat the process of drawing one bean from each cup and recording the result one hundred times. Be sure to return the beans to their respective cups and shake them after each drawing. These paired factors illustrate the way factors would join to form one hundred seeds of the next (F_2) generation.

   What would be the height of the plants produced by each of the seeds whose factors you recorded? How many will be tall? How many will be short? Based on your data, what percentage of the F_2 generation will be tall? What percentage will be short? Of those that are tall, what percentage will be true-breeding—have only the hereditary factors for tallness (two dark beans)? (Such plants are said to be homozygous because both factors are the same.) Notice that all the short plants are homozygous. What percentage will have a factor for both tall and short (*Tt:* one dark bean, and one light-colored bean)? Such plants are said to be heterozygous.

10. How do the percentages of tall and short plants in the F_2 generation that you obtained in your experiment compare with Mendel's results (see Table 2)? Why might your percentages be different from his?

EXPERIMENT 18

THE ROLE OF PROBABILITY IN HEREDITY

To see how expected results may be modified by probability, you can do a simple experiment.

1. Use two pennies, one bright and one tarnished (dull), to represent gametes from two members of

THINGS YOU WILL NEED

- **2 pennies, one bright and shiny and one tarnished and dull**
- **a partner**
- **pen or pencil**
- **notebook**

the heterozygous F_1 generation (Tt). The head's side of the bright penny represents the dominant factor for tallness (T_1), its tail side represents the factor for shortness (t_1). Similarly, the head's side of the dull penny represents the tallness factor from a second plant (T_2); the tail's side represents the factor for shortness (t_2).

Each coin has the same chance of turning up heads as it does tails. Consequently, if the two coins are tossed at the same time, the probability of two heads can be expected in one-fourth of the trials. The same is true of two tails. That means a head matched with a tail can be expected in one-half the trials. Figure 18 shows why such outcomes can be expected.

2. Ask a partner to flip one of the pennies, while you flip the other at the same time. Let them fall to the floor. Then record the results in a data table like the one in Table 3. Use simple check marks like the ones shown to record the result of each toss of the coins.

After twelve tosses, what would you expect the results to be? How many times would you expect both coins to be heads? Both tails? One heads and one tails?

What are the actual results? How do they compare with your prediction?

3. What are the results after fifty tosses of the two coins? After one hundred tosses? After two hundred tosses?

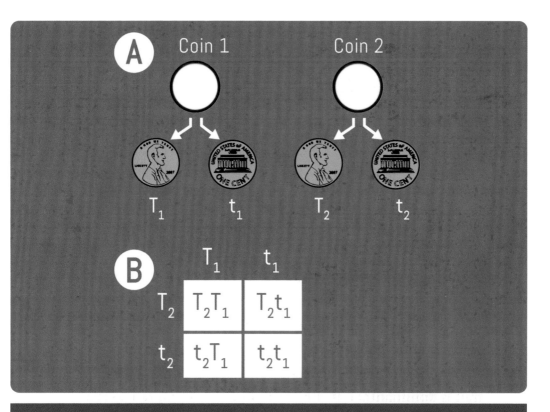

Figure 18. a) Two pennies are tossed. Each has an equal probability for landing heads or tails. b) One way to show the probabilities is to list the possibilities for one penny along a horizontal axis and the possibilities for the other penny along a vertical axis. As you can see, both coins can be expected to land heads up in one-fourth of the trials. The same is true for their both landing tails up. One heads and one tails can be expected in half the trials.

How does the number of tosses affect the actual results as compared to the expected results? Why do you think Mendel used hundreds of plants in his experiments? Why was Mendel's knowledge of mathematics useful to him in doing his experiments?

Table 3: A data table for recording the results of tossing two coins at the same time. The results of four hypothetical tosses are shown. The results of your first four tosses may be different.

Both heads (T_1T_2)	Both tails (t_1t_2)	Dull heads/ Bright tails (T_2t_1)	Bright heads/ Dull tails (T_1t_2)
√	√	√	√

ANOTHER OF MENDEL'S EXPERIMENTS

Mendel crossed plants homozygous for green pods with plants homozygous for yellow pods. His results revealed that all members of the F_1 generation had green pods. Which trait is dominant?

When members of the F_1 generation were crossed, the F_2 generation showed a ratio of three plants with green pods for every one plant with yellow pods. Make a Punnett square to show the results of crossing pure-bred plants that had yellow pods with pure-bred plants that had green pods. Make another Punnett square to show the F_1 cross.

Mendel wondered what would happen if he examined two pairs of hereditary factors through several generations of pea plants. Would they behave as separate factors or would they stick together?

To find out, he crossed true-breeding tall plants that had green pods with true-breeding short plants that had yellow pods. He found that all the plants in the F_1 generation were tall and bore green pods. The results did not surprise him because tallness and green-colored pods were both dominant traits.

When he crossed plants from the F_1 generation, he found that 9/16 of the F_2 plants were tall and had green pods, 3/16 were tall with yellow pods, 3/16 were short with green pods, and 1/16 had both recessive traits. They were short and had yellow pods. This was a ratio of 9:3:3:1.

EXPERIMENT 19

MODELING THE INHERITANCE OF TWO INDEPENDENT TRAITS

Mendel was not surprised by the results of his experiment. Were you? See if you can develop a model to explain the 9:3:3:1 ratio he obtained in the F_2 generation. Remember, in his P_1 generation, plants homozygous for tallness and green pods were crossed with short plants that had yellow pods. Then compare your model with his.

THINGS YOU WILL NEED

- **48 dry dark beans and 48 dry light-colored beans of the same size and shape**
- **48 dry green split peas and 48 dry yellow split peas**
- **4 paper cups**
- **pen or pencil and notebook**

1. Compare your model with Mendel's results. Mendel assumed that hereditary factors are independent of one another and are passed independently to the next generation through the plant's gametes. To see how this works, once again represent the factor for tall plants with dark beans and the factor for short plants with light-colored

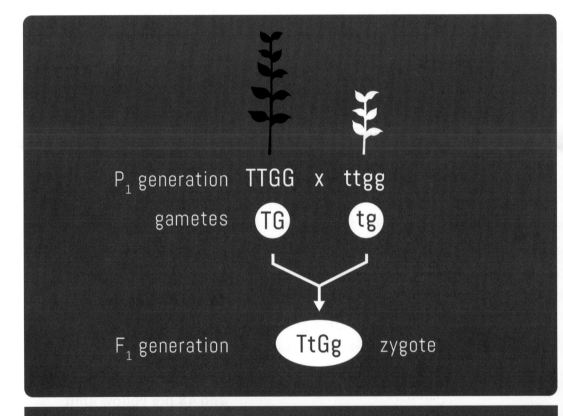

Figure 19. This diagram shows a cross between plants homozygous for tallness (*TT*) and green pods (*GG*) with plants homozygous for shortness (*tt*) and yellow pods (*gg*). Gametes from one set of plants carry the factors *t* and *g*. Gametes from the other group of plants carry the factors *T* and *G*. The F_1 generation will all be tall with green pods. However, they will be heterozygous for these traits (*TtGg*). What types of gametes will the F_1 generation produce (*TtGg* x *TtGg*)?

beans. Dry, green split peas can be used to represent the dominant factor for green pods. Dry, yellow split peas can be used to represent the recessive factor for yellow pods.

2. From Experiment 18, you know that the F_1 generation will be heterozygous for both height (Tt) and pod color (Gg). T represents the factor for tallness, t the factor for shortness. Let G represent the dominant factor for green pods and g the recessive factor for yellow pods. Figure 19 shows the gametes produced by the P_1 plants and the factors found in the F_1 generation, where all the plants are heterozygous for height and pod color.

3. Now make a model of the factors for height and pod color in the F_1 plants. Place two dozen dark beans and an equal number of light-colored beans in the same paper cup (cup 1). Do the same with a second cup (cup 2). Cover the cups with your hand and shake them to thoroughly mix the seeds. The two kinds of beans represent the hereditary factors for height that can be in a gamete from an F_1 pea plant. The reason for the two cups is that one factor for height comes from each of two parents.

4. Add two dozen dry, green split peas and an equal number of dry, yellow split peas to a third paper cup (cup 3). Do the same with a fourth cup (cup 4). Cover the cups with your hand and shake them to thoroughly mix the seeds.

5. Put cup 1 with beans and cup 3 with split peas next to one another. Place cups 2 and 4 close to one another but apart from the first two. Pair 1 and 3 and pair 2 and 4 contain the factors for height and pod color present in a parent. The "gametes" from these two parents will be joined to form the seeds of the F_2 generation. Each gamete will contain a hereditary factor for height and pod color.

6. Close your eyes. Then reach into a cup that holds the different colored beans. Remove one bean from the cup. Do the same for the cup next to it that contains the two types of split peas. Put these two "hereditary factors" together. They represent the factors for height and pod color that will be in a gamete from one parent. Similarly, join the hereditary factors for height and pod color that will be in a gamete from the second parent. Mendel assumed, as you have, that each seed receives one factor for height and one factor for pod color from each parent as shown by the Punnett square in Figure 20.

Any organism has both a phenotype and a genotype. Its phenotype is its appearance, the way it looks. Its genotype is its genetic makeup, the genes it contains. For example, suppose you have a pea plant that inherited factors for tallness and yellow pods from one parent (*Tg*) and factors for shortness and green pods from the other (*tG*). The plant's phenotype is tall with green pods. Its genotype with respect

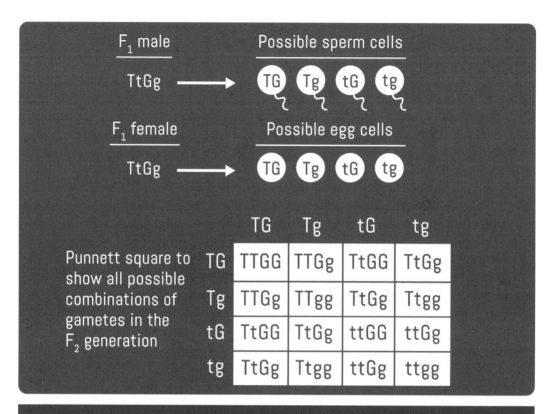

Figure 20. The F₁ generation is heterozygous for height and pod color (*TtGg*). They can produce four types of gametes for these two traits. The Punnett square shows the gametes and the factors in the sixteen possible types of seeds that can form when gametes from the parents unite. What fraction of the F₂ plants can be expected to be tall with green pods? Tall with yellow pods? Short with green pods? Short with yellow pods?

to height and pod color is *TtGg* (heterozygous tall and heterozygous for green pods).

Record the phenotype and genotype of the plant that will be produced by the "gametes" you have just joined.

7. Put the beans and peas back in the cups from which they came. Cover the cups and shake them to mix the seeds.

8. Repeat the process ninety-nine more times so that you will have the results of one hundred different unions of gametes. Record phenotype and genotype for each trial.

9. Examine your results. Will any of the seeds produce plants that are short with yellow pods? If so, what fraction of the one hundred plants has both these recessive traits? What fraction will be tall and have green pods? What fraction will be tall with yellow pods? What fraction will be short and have green pods?

How closely do your results agree with the 9:3:3:1 phenotype ratio that Mendel expected from the cross *TtGg* x *TtGg*?

HUMAN BLOOD TYPES

Our red blood cells (erythrocytes), which contain hemo-globin, transport oxygen from our lungs to the cells of our bodies. These blood cells may carry a substance—an "antigen." These antigens, known as A and B, are chemical compounds that, when present, cause antibodies to form. The antibodies, known as anti-A and anti-B, react with a specific antigen. The anti-A antibody reacts with the A anti-gen; the anti-B antibody reacts with the B antigen.

An individual's red blood cells may contain one, both, or neither of these two antigens. Human blood, therefore, can be one of four types—A, B, AB, or O. As you can see from

Table 4, a person with type A blood has the A antigen on his or her red blood cells; a person with type B blood has the B antigen; someone with type AB blood has both antigens; and a person with type O blood has neither antigen. Blood serum (the fluid part of blood that remains after blood clots) may contain antibodies that react with the A or B antigens, causing the blood cells to clump together (agglutinate).

Agglutination can be seen through a microscope. Consequently, a person's blood type can be readily determined. A person with type AB blood has neither antibody. If she did, her antibodies would react with the antigens on her own red blood cells, causing agglutination. Agglutinated cells would be unable to flow through small blood vessels and the person would die. Consequently, a person's blood type must be known before a blood transfusion takes place.

Table 4: The four blood types and the antigens on the red blood cells (RBCs) and the antibodies in the blood serum.

Blood type	Antigens on RBC	Antibodies in serum
A	A	Anti-B
B	B	Anti-A
AB	A and B	Neither antibody
O	Neither antigen	Anti-A and Anti-B

To determine a person's blood type, a small amount of his or her blood is placed on each of two glass slides. A drop of blood serum containing the anti-A antibody is added to one drop; a drop of serum containing the anti-B antibody is added to the other drop. Table 5 shows how a person's blood type can be determined by simply adding the anti-A and anti-B serum to a sample of that person's blood. Someone with type A blood has the A-antigen and the anti-B antibodies. Her red blood cells will clump when anti-A serum is added but not when anti-B serum is added. Type B blood, which contains the B-antigen, will clump when anti-B serum is added but not when anti-A serum is added. Either anti-A or anti-B will cause type AB blood to clump. On the other hand, a person with type O blood carries both antibodies but neither antigen on his red blood cells. Therefore, his blood cells will not clump when blood serum with either antibody is added. That is why people with type O blood are said to be universal blood donors.

The percentages of the people in the United States who have one of four blood types are found in Table 6. As you can see, type O is the most common and type AB is the rarest.

Table 5: Typing blood by adding a known antiserum to the blood in question. A + sign indicates agglutination; a– sign indicates no agglutination.

Anti-A serum added to the blood sample	Anti-B serum added to the blood sample	Test indicates antigen on the RBC is	Test indicates blood is type
+	−	A	A
−	+	B	B
+	+	A and B	AB
−	−	neither	O

Table 6: Percentage of the population that is of each blood type.

Blood type	Percentage of people with that blood type
AB	3
B	9
A	42
O	46

In addition to the A, B, AB, and O blood types, humans possess other blood antigens for which tests have been developed. For example, people may be either Rh positive (85 percent) or Rh negative (15 percent); they may be type M, type N, or type MN.

Considering all the possible combinations of blood types and enzymes, an individual may be quite unique. For example, the probability of having both type AB and Rh negative blood is 0.03 x 0.15 = 0.0045 or 4.5 people per thousand. If other blood factors are considered, the probability of finding someone with identical blood may be extremely small.

INHERITANCE OF HUMAN BLOOD TYPES

Because blood tests are so common, most people know their blood type. That knowledge will be important as you do this experiment.

1. Obtain the blood types of as many people who are related to one another as possible. Start with your own family.

2. What is your blood type? What are the blood types of your brothers and sisters? What are your parents' blood types? Your grandparents? Your great grandparents? Record all your data. It should include the blood type (O, A, B, or AB) of each person and the relationships of the people involved.

3. If possible, investigate the blood types of other people who are related. Record all that data as well.

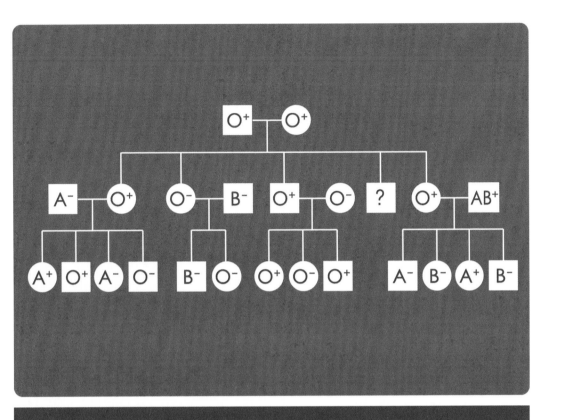

Figure 21. A family tree shows blood types A, B, AB, and O; and Rh+ or Rh−.

4. One investigation might provide data like that found in the family tree shown in Figure 21. What, if anything, can you conclude about the inheritance of blood type from the evidence in Table 7? Do any of the data in Figure 21 conflict with yours?

5. Geneticists who have studied the inheritance of blood types among humans have found that if both parents are Rh negative, all their children will be Rh negative.

In some marriages where both parents are Rh positive, all the children are Rh positive. In other such marriages some of their offspring may be Rh negative. In some marriages where one parent is Rh positive and the other Rh negative, all the children are Rh positive. In other such marriages, some of the children will be Rh positive and some will be Rh negative. All this suggests that the gene for Rh positive blood is dominant to the gene for Rh negative blood.

Table 7 summarizes the inheritance of blood types. It shows what blood types may appear in the children of parents having various blood types. Does the data in the table agree with what you found?

How are blood types inherited? Which gene or genes are recessive? Dominant? Codominant?

GENES, CHROMOSOMES, AND MODELS

In 1900, Hugo de Vries, a Dutch botanist, had been studying the inherited traits of primroses. He observed that every once in a while a new variety of primrose differing significantly from others would suddenly appear and reproduce. De Vries had discovered the cause of evolution. The sudden appearance of new traits was called a mutation. Experiments demonstrated that a mutation, which appeared in one member of a species, could be transmitted to its offspring. If the change provided an adaptation that enabled the organisms to better cope with their environment, then they were more

Table 7: The inheritance of blood types based on results from a large group of families.

Blood type of parents	Blood types that may appear in children	Blood types that do not appear in children
O x O	O	A, B, AB
O x A	O, A	B, AB
O x B	O, B	A, AB
O x AB	A, B	O, AB
A x A	A, O	B, AB
A x B	O, A, B, AB	—
A x AB	A, B, AB	O
B x B	O, B	A, AB
B x AB	A, B, AB	O
AB x AB	A, B, AB	O

likely to survive than other members of the species. Over time, the accumulation of mutations could lead to a new species. Mendel discovered the basic manner in which traits are transmitted from generation to generation. De Vries discovered mutations, the explanation for variation within a species that Darwin sought.

CHROMOSOMES AND GENES

As microscopes improved, biologists began to observe details inside plant and animal cells. Most cells contained a spherical object that was called the nucleus. Surrounding the

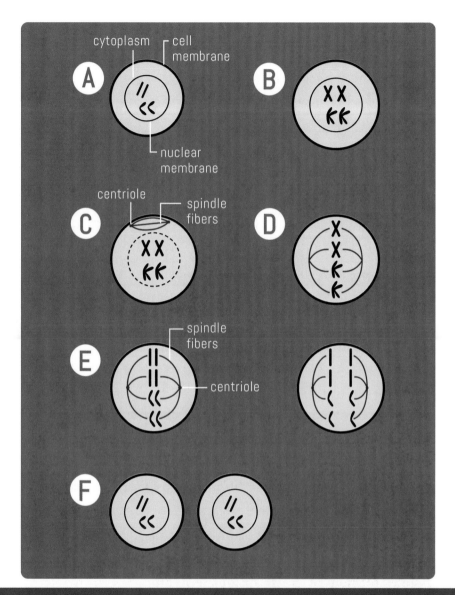

Figure 22. Mitosis is the duplication of chromosomes in a cell's nucleus during cell division. As a result of mitosis, each daughter cell receives the same number and type of chromosomes as the parent cell. This diagram shows a cell with two pairs of chromosomes. a) A cell before mitosis begins. b) Each chromosome replicates. c) The nuclear membrane disappears and spindle fibers form. d) Spindle fibers attach to the chromosomes lined up in the center of the cell. e) The chromosomes separate and move to opposite sides of the cell. f) The cell divides, nuclear membranes form, and two daughter cells now exist, each with the same chromosomes as the parent cell.

nucleus was the jelly-like cytoplasm. And while the cytoplasm of muscle, nerve, connective, blood, and epithelial cells was quite different, their nuclei were similar.

In 1880, Walther Flemming, a German scientist, found that material within the nuclei of cells absorbed a red dye he was using to stain cells. He called the string-like material chromatin, from the Greek word for "color" (*khrōma*). He could see the chromatin at different stages of cell division. He found that as a cell began to divide, the chromatin became shorter and thicker forming what came to be known as chromosomes. Flemming was able to observe the chromosomes at different stages of cell division, a process he called mitosis.

During mitosis, the membrane surrounding the nucleus breaks down and thin fibers known as spindle fibers form and attach to the chromosomes. As Figure 22 shows, each chromosome replicates (copies itself) so that the number of chromosomes doubles. The duplicates then separate as they are pulled to opposite sides of the cell forming two new cells each with the same number of chromosomes as the parent cell.

Biologists who studied mitosis were puzzled. If gametes have the same number of chromosomes as other cells, the zygotes formed by the union of sperm and egg cells would have twice as many chromosomes as their parents. Since all the cells of an organism appeared to come from the repeated mitotic division of the zygote, the number of chromosomes in the cells would double in each successive generation.

MEIOSIS

Careful observations of the cell divisions that occur during the formation of gametes provided an answer. Gametes, unlike other cells, are formed by a different type of cell division—a process that came to be known as meiosis. During meiosis, only one member of each pair of chromosomes reaches a sperm or egg cell (see Figure 23). Consequently, the number of chromosomes in the gametes is half the number found in other cells. When gametes unite to form a zygote, the chromosomes pair off

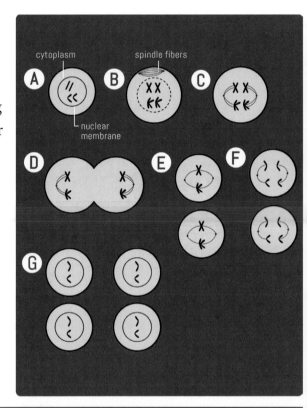

Figure 23. During meiosis each gamete receives only one member of each pair of chromosomes found in the other cells of the body. Human cells have forty-six chromosomes (twenty-three pairs). Human sperm and egg cells have twenty-three chromosomes. a) The parent cells that give rise to the gametes have the typical number of chromosomes for the species. b) Each chromosome replicates as the nuclear membrane disappears and spindle fibers form. c) The chromosomes line up in matching pairs on the cell's equator. d) One pair of each of the matching pairs of chromosomes is pulled to opposite sides of the cell. e) Chromosomes in the daughter cells line up and attach to spindle fibers. f) Each pair of chromosomes in the daughter cells separates and goes to opposite sides of the cell. g) The cells divide to form gametes. Each gamete has only one member of each pair of chromosomes.

again and the number of chromosomes per cell is restored to the number typical of the species. For humans, that number is forty-six (twenty-three pairs).

The discovery of chromosomes provided biologists with the actual matter that could transmit inherited traits from parents to offspring. The chromosomes, it was later discovered, were believed to be made up of smaller chemical units, called genes, which were the source of all inherited traits. The factors for the yellow or green color of peas, the height of the pea plants, the color of human eyes, and all other inherited characteristics were transmitted by genes found along the chromosomes in the nuclei of gametes.

EXPERIMENT 21

A LOOK AT CHROMOSOMES

If possible, obtain prepared microscope slides that have been stained to reveal different stages of mitosis and meiosis. The most commonly used cells are from onions, ascaris (roundworms), and

THINGS YOU WILL NEED

- **prepared slides of mitosis and meiosis**
- **microscope**

whitefish. You may be able to borrow such slides and a microscope from your school's science department.

1. Examine slides of mitosis. Can you see cells in which there is a distinct nuclear membrane and strands of chromatin? If you can, you are observing a cell not yet undergoing cell division. This step in cell division is called interphase.

2. Cells in which the nuclear membrane disappears and spindle fibers are evident are in prophase.

3. If you see chromosomes lined up near the cell's equator and attached to the spindle fibers, the cell is in metaphase. Can you see spindle fibers during metaphase?

4. Can you detect cells where the chromosomes are separating and being pulled to opposite sides of the cell? These cells are in anaphase.

5. In the last phase of cell division, known as telophase, the chromosomes are clustered at opposite sides of a cell and a new cell membrane is forming between them. The result is two daughter cells. What differences would you expect to find between cells undergoing mitosis as compared with those undergoing meiosis?

A MODEL OF MITOSIS

A model is helpful in under-standing what happens to chromosomes during mitosis. You can use pipe cleaners or twist-ties to represent chromosomes.

> **THINGS YOU WILL NEED**
>
> - **12 pipe cleaners or twist-ties to represent chromosomes**
> - **colored felt-tip pen**
> - **sheet of paper**

1. On a sheet of paper, draw a large circle to represent a cell.
2. Prepare a model of four (two pairs) chromosomes as shown in Figure 24a. Bend the tips of one pair. Color one member of each pair with a felt-tip pen so you can distinguish it from its twin.
3. Line up the "chromosomes," one after the other, along the equator of the cell you drew on paper. These figures represent the metaphase part of mitosis as shown in Figure 24b.
4. At this point the chromosomes replicate. Consequently, use pipe cleaners and a colored felt-tip pen to prepare four more chromosomes identical to

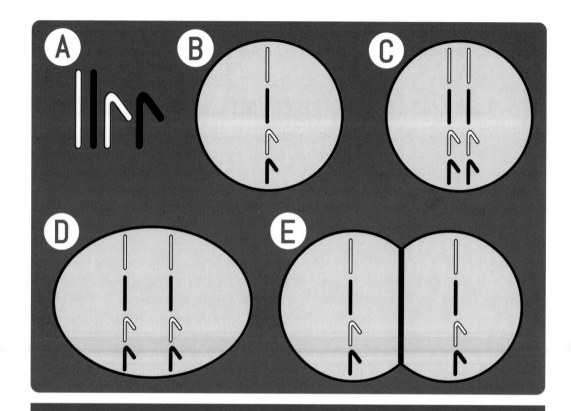

Figure 24. Pipe cleaners or twist-ties can be used to model chromosomes in cells undergoing mitosis.

the first four. Place them next to their identical partners as shown in Figure 24c.

5. Next, separate the identical chromosomes as occurs
during the anaphase part of mitosis (Figure 24d).

6. Finally (Figure 24e), draw a thick line between the
separated chromosomes to show that cell division has
occurred.

How do the number of chromosomes in the
two new cells compare with the number that were

in the original cell? How do the number of pairs of chromosomes in the two new cells compare with the number that were in the original nucleus?

If these pipe cleaners or twist-ties represent the number of chromosomes characteristic of a particular species, how many pairs of chromosomes are in each body cell of a member of this species? How many chromosomes will be found in the gametes produced by this species? How many members of each pair of chromosomes will be in the gametes of this species?

EXPERIMENT 23

A MODEL OF MEIOSIS

A physical model is even more helpful in understanding what happens to chromosomes during meiosis when sperm or egg cells are produced. Pipe cleaners or twist-ties can, again, represent chromosomes, but you will need twice as many.

THINGS YOU WILL NEED

- **24 pipe cleaners or twist-ties to represent chromosomes**
- **pieces of colored yarn, preferably green, yellow, and dark**
- **sheets of paper**
- **pen or pencil**

1. Prepare four (two pairs) model chromosomes. Do this twice so that you have a total of eight chromosomes as shown in Figure 25a.
2. Attach a small piece of green yarn to one member of each pair of the straight chromosomes. The yarn will represent the gene for green pod color.
3. To the mate in each pair, at a corresponding place, attach a small piece of yellow yarn to represent the gene for yellow pod color.
4. To one member of each pair of the hook-shaped chromosomes attach a *long* piece of dark yarn to represent the gene for tallness.
5. To its mate in each pair, at a corresponding place, attach a *short* piece of dark yarn to represent the gene for shortness.

      These are the "genes" and "chromosomes" that would be present in the F1 generation following a cross of pea plants homozygous for green pods and tallness with short plants that produce yellow pods.
6. On a sheet of paper, draw two large circles to represent two cells.
7. Line up the chromosomes in pairs along the equator of each cell to represent the metaphase part of meiosis. (Remember, in meiosis the chromosomes are paired during metaphase. As you can see from Figure 25b and 25b', the two pairs of chromosomes can line up in two different ways. The straight chromosome with the gene for green pods can be on the same side of the equator as the hook-shaped chromosome

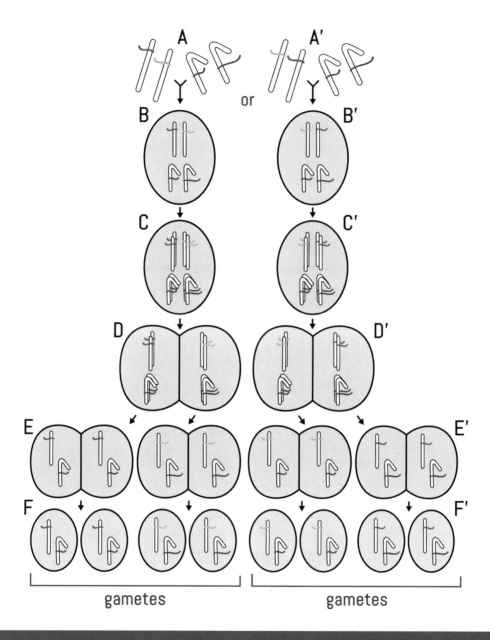

Figure 25. During meiosis one member of each pair of chromosomes enters each gamete. This is accomplished by two cell divisions. Only during the first cell division do the chromosomes replicate.

carrying the gene for tallness or on the same side as the one that carries the gene for shortness.

8. During the metaphase of meiosis, the chromosomes replicate themselves forming four-chromosome clusters (known as tetrads) around the equator of the cell. Use pipe cleaners or twist-ties and colored yarn to prepare eight more chromosomes identical to the first eight.

9. Place them next to their identical partners as shown in Figure 25c and 25c'.

10. Next, separate the identical chromosomes as happens during the anaphase part of the first meiotic cell division (Figure 25d and 25d'). Draw a line between the separated chromosomes to show that the cell has divided.

    If cell division stopped here, how many chromosomes would be in the gametes (sperm or egg cells)? How many chromosomes would be in the zygote formed by the union of sperm and egg cells? What would happen to the number of chromosomes in the cells of the organism in each succeeding generation?

11. The second cell division in meiosis reduces the chromosome number to half the number found in the other cells of the organism. To see how this happens, separate the chromosomes you have in each cell after the first cell division (Figure 25d and 25d'). Move them to opposite sides of a cell nucleus and draw a line to represent cell division as shown

in Figure 25e and 25e'. This represents the second meiotic division.

12. Finally, place the chromosomes in cells that have separated into four distinct "gametes" as shown in Figure 25f and 25f'.

How do the number of chromosomes in the gametes compare with the number that were in the original parent cell prior to meiosis? How many members of each pair of chromosomes are in each of the gametes? How many distinct types of gametes are there? How many would there be in a species that has four pairs of chromosomes? Humans have twenty-three pairs of chromosomes. How many chromosomes would you expect to find in human egg or sperm cells?

EXPLORING ON YOUR OWN

- Use your hands and those of a friend to make a model of chromosomes during the two cell divisions that constitute meiosis.
- Pea plants that are homozygous tall with yellow pods are crossed with short pea plants that are homozygous for green pods. Use a chromosome model to show that in the F_2 generation you can expect to find plants in a ratio of 9 tall with green pods:3 tall with yellow pods: 3 short with green pods:1 short with yellow pods.
- Use chromosome models to show that the traits Mendel studied—height, seed shape, color of the seed leaves, seed coats, pod shape, pod color, and position of pods on the stem—must have been located on different chromosomes.
- Is there any evidence to suggest that it may be possible to make artificial chromosomes? If it did become possible, would it offer any benefits to humans?

SEX DETERMINATION: MALE OR FEMALE

What determines the sex of a human? The explanation came from a microscopic examination of the chromosomes in fruit flies. Geneticists noticed that one pair of chromosomes in male fruit flies was different from that pair in female flies (see Figure 26). Later it was discovered that in humans the chromosomes in one of the twenty-three pairs differ in

Figure 26. The chromosomes found in female fruit flies are shown on the left. Those found in males are shown on the right. Both have four pairs of chromosomes. But in the males the chromosomes in one pair are not similar. The hook-shaped chromosome is found only in male flies. It is called the Y chromosome.

shape. Again, it was the males who had the dissimilar chromosome, which came to be known as the Y chromosome. Thus, females in both fruit flies and humans have two X chromosomes, while males have one X and one Y chromosome. In some species, the male has no Y chromosome but simply one X chromosome.

A MODEL OF HOW SEX IS DETERMINED IN HUMANS

To better understand how the sex of a baby is determined you can develop a model.

> **THINGS YOU WILL NEED**
>
> - **8 pipe cleaners or twist-ties**
> - **sheets of paper**

1. Place two pipe cleaners or twist-ties side by side on a sheet of paper as shown in Figure 27a. These two pipe cleaners or twist-ties represent the two X chromosomes in the cells of a prospective mother.

2. On another sheet of paper, place two more pipe cleaners or twist-ties. Bend one of these pipe cleaners or twist-ties as shown in Figure 27a to represent the Y chromosome found paired with an X chromosome in the cells of a prospective father.

   During meiosis, as you know, only one member of each pair of chromosomes enters the gametes (eggs or sperm cells) produced in the ovaries or testes. (In Figure 27b, c, and d, both cell divisions in meiosis are shown.)

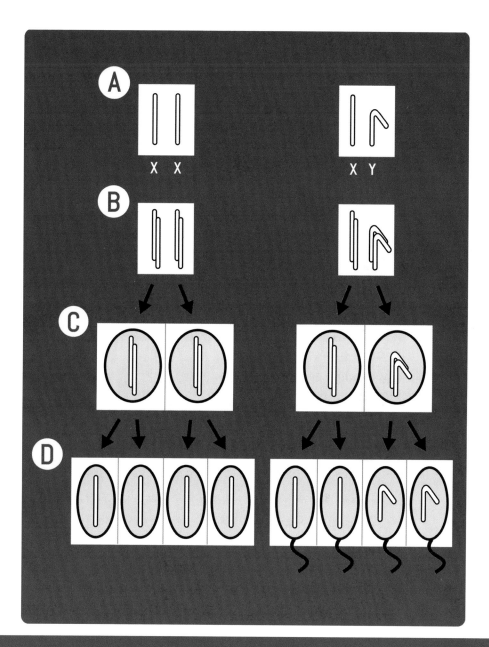

Figure 27. a) The two unbent strips represent the chromosomes in the cells of a potential mother. The bent strip represents the Y chromosome in the cells of a potential father. During meiosis as gametes form, the cells divide twice, and each gamete receives only one member of each pair of chromosomes. Each egg receives an X chromosome. Half the sperm cells receive an X chromosome. The other half receive a Y chromosome. Which chromosome did you receive, X or Y?

3. To form a model of the process, separate the chromosomes so that each gamete receives only one chromosome from the pair.
4. What fraction of the sperm cells receive an X chromosome? What fraction receive a Y chromosome?
5. Use your model to follow the X and Y chromosomes when an egg and a sperm cell unite to form a zygote. Is it the male gamete or the female gamete that determines the sex of the offspring?

GLOSSARY

biological classification A scientific way to name a species. The name has two parts: its genus name, which is capitalized, and its species name, which is not. For example the human species is *Homo sapiens*. Both the genus and species names are italicized.

blind spot A point at the back of the eye where the optic nerve passes through the retina. There are no nerve receptors there. Consequently, any light or image striking that spot cannot be seen.

blood types Humans have blood types that are inherited. There are four—O, A, B, and AB as well as Rh negative and Rh positive.

chromosomes Thread-like structures in a cell's nucleus that contain protein and DNA (deoxriboynucleic acid). For example, in a pea plant, the genes (factors) that control visible traits such as color, size, and seed shape are located on chromosomes.

convex lens A lens near the front of the eye that refracts (bends) light to form images on the retina.

gamete One of the cells that will unite together to start to make a new organism. Egg cells and sperm cells are both gametes.

homologous organs Bones and organs that have the same embryonic origin and basic structure even though they serve different purposes. An example is the arm of a human and the wing of a bird.

humerus The upper bone of the human arm and the wing of a chicken.

meiosis Cell division leading to the formation of gametes that have half the number of chromosomes as other cells of the body. The union of gametes to form zygotes restores the chromosome number found in other cells of the body.

mitosis Cell division when the chromosomes replicate and then divide forming two cells, each containing the same number of chromosomes.

photosynthesis A process in which green plants combine carbon dioxide and water in the presence of light to produce food and oxygen.

pulse The expansion of arteries as blood is forced through them by the pumping heart.

radius and ulna The two bones of the lower arm.

retina The lining, rich in sensory cells, at the back of the eyes.

seeds Seeds form when ova in a flower's pistil are fertilized by sperm from a flower's stamens. The seeds contain the plant's embryos and will germinate (mature) under proper conditions.

zygote The resulting cell that is created when an egg cell and a sperm cell unite.

FURTHER READING

BOOKS

Ardley, Neil. *101 Great Science Experiments*. New York, NY: DK Ltd., 2014.

Gotlieb, Avrum I. *Planning a Career in Biomedical and Life Sciences: Making Informed Choices.* Cambridge, MA: Academic Press, 2014.

Henneberg, Susan. *Creating Science Fair Projects With Cool New Digital Tools*. New York, NY: Rosen Central, 2014.

Hetland Beth. *Backyard Biology.* White River Junction, VT: Nomad Press, 2013.

Hovey, Tim E. *Out in the Field: Discovering a Career in Field Biology.* CreateSpace Independent Publishing Platform, 2012.

Thompson, Robert Bruce, and Barbara Fritchman Thompson. *Illustrated Guide to Home Biology Experiments: All Lab, No Lecture.* San Francisco, CA: Maker Media, 2012.

VanCleave, Janice. *Step-by-Step Experiments in Biology.* New York, NY: Rosen, 2013.

Willett, Edward. *Infectious Disease Specialists: Hunting Down Disease*. New York, NY: Enslow Publishing, 2016.

WEBSITES

American Society of Plant Biologists
my.aspb.org
Learn more about plant biology.

Exploratorium: Science Snacks
exploratorium.edu/snacks/subject/biology
Check out the biology demonstrations and scientific facts.

Kids.gov: Plants
kids.usa.gov/science/plants
Click on the links to plant facts, experiments, and information from experts in plant biology.

CAREER INFORMATION

American Institute of Biological Sciences

aibs.org/careers

Read about careers in biology and click on further links.

Big Future

bigfuture.collegeboard.org/majors-careers

This career- and job-based website has a focus on college
   majors.

Salary.com

www1.salary.com/biologist-I-Salaries.html

Find information on a variety of careers in biology.

Science Pioneers

sciencepioneers.org/students/stem-websites

This resource has links to various STEM career websites.

INDEX

A

Amphibia, 32
Angiospermae, 35
Animalia, 30
Archaea, 31
Artiodactyla, 33
Aves, 32

B

Bacteria, 31
biologists
  definition, 6
  preparing to be a, 6–7
  types of, 8–9
  working as a, 8–9
blood, circulation of, 16–18
blood types, human, 94–97
  inheritance of, 98–100
bone structure, mammalian,
  47–57

C

carbon dioxide
  in animals, 17
  use by plants, 31, 42, 45–47

Carnivora, 33
Cetacea, 33
Chiroptera, 32
chlorophyll, 31, 42, 44
chromosomes, 76, 100–101,
  101–103, 104–105,
  105–106, 107–109,
  109–110, 112–113, 114,
  115, 116, 118
class, 30
classification
  of animals, 31–34
  biological, 27–31
  of plants, 35–37
convex lens, model of, 23–25

D

Darwin, Charles, 59, 60, 61,
  63, 65, 66, 67, 69, 73,
  74, 75, 76, 101
dissection, 38
domain, 30, 31, 33

E

Eukarya, 30, 31
evolution, theory of, 59–60

T

U

V

Z